Early Supports for Family Life:
A Social Work Experiment

by: Ludwig L. Geismar
Bruce Lagay
Isabel Wolock
Ursula C. Gerhart
Harriet Fink

Social Work Research Center
Graduate School of Social Work
Rutgers University

The Scarecrow Press, Inc., Metuchen, N.J., 1972

Copyright 1972 by Ludwig L. Geismar

Library of Congress Cataloging in Publication Data
Main entry under title:

Early supports for family life.

    Includes bibliographical references.
    1. Family social work. I. Geismar, Ludwig L.
HV43.E2   362.8'2   70-188615
ISBN 0-8108-0476-X

Contents

List of Tables

iv

v

Acknowledgments

An action-research endeavor such as the Family Life Improvement Project owes a debt of gratitude to many people. Unquestionably, our primary thanks go to the families who consented to participate in the enterprise and particularly to the 352 parents who with their children remained in the study for a full five years. We are also heavily indebted to eight social workers, Richard Anderson, Mildred Badanes, Anne Cohen, Josephine Green, Lillian Haber, Barbara Ann Hill, Susan Moses, and Esther Stavis, who rendered imaginative and conscientious service to the families in the treatment group; and to the research interviewers, Audrey Green, Sara Holzer, and Jackie O'Brien, who unhesitatingly went out to collect data at odd hours, in bad weather, and in areas even local residents termed unsafe. The data analysis would have been unfeasible without the responsible work of the research coders, Zona Fishkin, Dorothy Jaker, Patricia Lagay, Judy Schwartz, Tammy Bezinew, Ruth Weingartner, Barry Camson and Bill Milmoe. And the whole operation benefited immeasurably from the devoted efforts of the clerical staff composed of Adele Verzatt, Louise Cerretani, Katria Harris, and Leona Thomas.

Special thanks are due to the Child Service Association of Newark and its dynamic director, Dr. Leontine Young, for providing the project with ample facilities in a setting conducive to research and practice. The contributions of Professor Jane Krisberg, director of the action program between 1965 and 1968, are gratefully acknowledged. Thanks are also due Professors Barry Indik and Paul Lerman for a careful reading of the manuscript and valuable suggestions for revisions. The responsibility for errors, however, is exclusively that of the authors. We are particularly thankful to Shirley Geismar for her careful editing of the manuscript and to Alix Cuilla for typing it.

Finally, we wish to express our deep appreciation to the U. S. Social and Rehabilitation Service for the generous financial support under Grant HEW #190, without which this project could not have come into existence.

L. L. G.   B. L.   I. W.   U. C. G.   H. F.

vi

Chapter 1

RESEARCH FOCUS ON YOUNG FAMILIES

Young families are rarely singled out as the subjects of service programs and evaluation studies. A society which puts a premium on self-sufficiency and non-dependence on psycho-social helping services sees little justification in serving those who are judged to have the greatest potential for making it on their own. The social helping services, in turn, are primarily geared to assisting people in distress. Although this is particularly true for psychiatry and clinical psychology, social work, whose primary method has been social casework, also tends to be heavily oriented toward the ameliorative approach or crisis intervention.

The decision to carry out an action-research project with young families emanated from a belief, admittedly in need of testing, that professional intervention with young families meets a need and can be effective. Although data relating family needs and problems to the age of the family are quite sparse, there is, nonetheless, converging evidence that the early child-rearing stages in the life cycle of the family are periods of increasing problemicity in social functioning. The need of young families for helping services resides less in the frequency and severity of their problems than in the fact that the early stage of the family life cycle appears to be one of dynamic change in the direction of more problematic social functioning. The writings of a number of researchers appear to give support to this thesis.

Lewis M. Terman, for instance, found in 1938 that marital happiness scores of couples dip to a low point after about seven years of marriage, only to rise again and reach a new low after 16 years of married life.[1] Dentler and Pineo followed up a Burgess and Wallin sample 20 years after marriage and observed that intimacy had been reduced and shared activities had decreased.[2] Blood and Wolfe, using cross-sectional analysis of family groups at different life-cycle stages, found a decline in love and marital companionship in each child-rearing stage.[3]

7

Eleanor Braun Luckey, likewise, found marital satisfaction negatively related to the number of years of marriage.[4]
Using checklists of personality variables she found that the
longer couples were married the less favorable personality
quality they see in their mates. Harold Feldman, who has
been studying marital communication, found that children
tend to reduce the interaction of spouses, and that both the
intimacy and intensity of the marital relationship declines
over the years.[5] Two recent studies relating marital satisfaction to family life cycle yielded findings which, though
contradictory in some aspects, agreed on a decrease in
satisfaction after the arrival of the first child which extended into the school-aged-children stage of the family life
cycle. Rollins and Feldman found the dependent-children
stages associated with negative evaluations of marriage,
particularly by the wife.[6] Wesley R. Burr, measuring six
types of marital satisfaction, found the school-age stage of
the family plagued with difficulties, but his data did not
support the hypothesis, based on the findings of other investigators, of a decrease in satisfaction from the early
stages of the family life cycle to the later stages.[7]

A cross-sectional study by Geismar, comparing the
social functioning of young families at two life-cycle stages,
revealed that families function better after the birth of the
first child than do families who have at least one child in
middle school (grades 6-8).[8] The present study has as
one of its aims the testing of the hypothesis, resting on the
evidence from the foregoing studies and others, that a deterioration in social functioning occurs during the years
following the birth of the first child. If this research yields
support of the hypothesis it may be argued that meeting a
need in young families can be defined as efforts which suc-
ceed in arresting or reversing the natural trend of deterioration in social functioning. Such effort may be termed primary prevention, a concept widely used in the field of public
health and deemed appropriate for application in the field of
social work as well[9] but rarely subjected to empirical testing.

The second reason possibly justifying a program of
services to young families is its hoped-for effectiveness,
although this most certainly remains to be demonstrated.
The hard evidence on the effectuality of remedial intervention
with families has not been very impressive, as we shall
show in a succeeding chapter. Limited success in dealing
with problematic families leaves much room for demonstra-
ting equal or better results with services to families which

have not, as a group, revealed patterns of serious malfunctioning.

There is yet another reason which would supply a
strong rationale for developing a service program especially
geared to the young family. That reason can be put under
the heading of humanizing the urban environment or finding
the means of enabling families, especially lower-class and
minority-group families, to become oriented to an increasingly
complex, specialized, and bureaucratized social structure.

A New York survey trying to determine the need for
a service which could help people get information and advice
on how to deal with the manifold problems of urban living
found that there was indeed a widespread need for such a
service.[10] But the need for actual resources to render
health, welfare, educational, and recreational services is
only one part of the larger problem which has another com-
ponent--the fact that urban residents do not know of existing
services and therefore do not make use of them.[11] The
American experience, in contrast to that of Britain which
supports a network of Citizens' Advice Bureaus,[12] is one in
which citizens feel disinclined to seek help with social problems because the American culture puts a premium on self-
sufficiency and independence. Furthermore, the social
service structure of recent decades has favored the motivated over the non-motivated client, an arrangement which
has worked greatly to the disadvantage of the lower classes
in American society.[13]

In the view of the writers a service to young families
marks a shift in social work emphasis from an exclusive
concern with remedial or problem oriented services to what
Alfred Kahn has termed developmental provisions.[14] Regardless of whether the developmental approach can be
proven to be preventive in the long run, its justification can
be based upon the value premise that society has as great a
responsibility to help those who are uninformed or alienated
or confused as those who are in serious trouble.

The design for the present action-research Project
envisions a service that reaches out to families rather than
one which waits to be sought out.[15] A new service as yet
unrooted in the mores of the population would seem to stand
little chance of being properly utilized unless ways were
found to bring the service to the people. It is one of the
assumptions of the study that once the service became known

and its value recognized by the people, the reaching-out endeavor would eventually give way to a seeking-out program which could function on a community or--in the case of large communities--neighborhood basis in a manner similar to that of the British Citizens' Advice Bureaus.

The overall design of the study makes it possible to employ action research in conjunction with the developmental approach in the study of families. The developmental frame of reference posits the time dimension as a significant variable in studying families for family life is viewed as a succession of life-cycle stages each of which is characterized by specific family norms, family roles, and family tasks. [16] The developmental conceptual framework encompasses the life cycle of the nuclear family of procreation from the wedding to the death of the spouses or the departure of children if they remain at home beyond the death of the parents. The family is viewed as a system of interacting individuals which changes over time due to changes in composition, age of family members, their psycho-social and economic needs, societal expectations for role performance at different life-cycle stages, etc. These stages have been delineated by various investigators in terms of such factors as common tasks and patterns of adjustment, and they range in number from as few as four identified by Sorokin, Zimmerman, and Galpin[17] to as many as 24 delineated by Roy H. Rodgers. [18]

In the research reported here interest centers on stages II (oldest child less than 30 months) and III (oldest child from 2 1/2 to six years of age) of the Duvall scheme.[19] Stage II, also termed the childbearing stage by Duvall, begins with the birth of the first child and represents a transition from childlessness to parenthood. This change calls for some major adjustments in the lives of the new parents (or the new mother if she is not married) as they pass from an existence involving the needs of two adults to one including responsibility for a third, completely dependent family member. Coupled with cultural pressures to ensure the assumption of the parental role is what Alice S. Rossi has termed the factor of irrevocability. [20] The relative freedom of choice which allows childless couples to continue the marriage or dissolve it gives way to a belief that the marital partnership is compelling and the responsibility for the offspring is irrevocable.

Parenthood has been depicted as a crisis in the life of the parents. [21] More recently the crisis notion has been

challenged,[22] and the belief has gained ground that the process of parenthood, though it requires some fundamental re-
adjustments in the lives of the marriage partners, is also a
period of marital satisfaction[23] accompanied by a strengthen-
ing of the husband-wife relationship.

The arrival of the first child generally increases the
family's financial obligations which take the form of larger
living quarters, medical bills for mother and child, and
food, clothing, furniture, and toys for the neonate. The
presence of the baby also necessitates a readjustment of the
social and recreational patterns of the parents who now must
do much of their planning with a helpless, dependent family
member in mind. The more formidable aspects of parenthood, however, reside in the process of child rearing and
for these guidelines are generally lacking.[24] "Parents can
readily inform themselves," says Rossi, "concerning the
young infant's nutritional, clothing and medical needs, and
follow the general prescription that a child needs loving
physical contact and emotional support."[25] Such advice
falls far short of supplying the parents with guidelines for
the successful socialization of children.

The problem of child care is likely to loom larger
during stage III of the family life cycle when the first infant has grown into a social being and interacts vigorously
with his environment while a sibling or two may already
have appeared on the scene, reducing the parent's ability
to give attention to the oldest one. The toddler or pre-
school child is apt to confront the parents with problems of
discipline and various forms of deviant behavior not found
in infants.

During the third life-cycle stage the rate of increase
in family size and concomitant rise in financial obligations
often runs ahead of the increase in the family's earning
power. This is especially true in situations where the main
wage earner is still undergoing vocational or professional
training or where he is employed in a bureaucratic enterprise whose salary structure only permits gradual advance-
ment which is unrelated to individual or family need.

Increased responsibility for child care and augmented
economic burdens make substantial demands upon the role
obligations of the marital partners. New roles emerge as
the family grows, old ones have to be modified or redefined
and in many instances reallocated between the partners. The

change in internal role structure is matched by role changes
in the community as a result of the family's moving to new
neighborhoods, dependence upon new community resources,
and the changing demands of extended family or kinship
groups.

The identification of developmental forces during the
second and third stages of the family life cycle can help
sensitize an observer to the existence of possible strains
and problems in family life which merit professional attention. These difficulties are not viewed as a universal occurrence or even as a characteristic of families in the early
stages of the life cycle. Their prevalence and incidence
needs to be determined by empirical study. Yet their pos-
tulation out of the context of the type of theoretical analysis
sketched above supplies a starting point for planning a program of professional intervention. Another vantage point
for the programming of services can be located by empirically analyzing the social functioning of a cohort of young
families in the early stages of the family life cycle. This
was done elsewhere and resulted in the formulation of a
strategy of early intervention[26] which was based on two
types of analysis: (1) A cross-sectional study of 216 families in stage II and (2) a comparison of a sub-group of
stage II families with a further sample of stage IV and V
families[27] (one or more children in middle school) living in
the same community. The former analysis was focused on
problems and needs of families at a given point in time;
the latter approach was designed to secure information about
changing problems and needs as these could be inferred from
changes in social functioning between two life-cycle stages.

The empirical model derived from the foregoing study
and the theoretical guidelines emanating from the developmental approach to family study were combined to formulate
a broad program of intervention to a representative group
of young, urban families. The program on the drawing
board took the form of a staff of social workers and supervisors and a set of guidelines, transmitted through close
supervision and in-service training, for rendering services
geared to what were perceived to be levels of functioning
and the developmental needs of the families to be served.

This service Project, unlike most social helping services, set out to test the general guidelines or model for
services against the services actually rendered to the young
families and to assess the effect of the program of

intervention on the social functioning of the families. The
next chapter, dealing with the design of the study, will first
take up the plan for the program of services, then review
the theoretical propositions underlying the method of measurement, and finally discuss sampling and data collection procedures.

Notes

1. Lewis M. Terman, Psychological Factors in Marital
   Happiness, New York: McGraw-Hill, 1938, p. 177.

2. Robert A. Dentler and Peter C. Pineo, "Sexual Adjust-
   ment, Marital Adjustment, and Personal Growth of
   Husbands, "Marriage and Family Living, Vol. 22,
   No. 1, February 1960, pp. 45-48.

3. Robert Blood and Donald M. Wolfe, Husbands and Wives,
   New York: Free Press, 1960.

4. Eleanor Braun Luckey, "Number of Years Married as
   Related to Personality Perception and Marital Satisfaction," Journal of Marriage and the Family, Vol.
   28, No. 1, February 1966, pp. 44-48.

5. Harold Feldman, Development of the Husband-Wife
   Relationship, Ithaca, N. Y. : Cornell University,
   Department of Child Development and Family Rela-
   tions, pp. 151-155 (mimeographed).

6. Boyd C. Rollins and Harold Feldman, "Marital Satisfaction Over the Family Life Cycle," Journal of
   Marriage and the Family, Vol. 32, No. 1, February
   1970, pp. 20-28.

7. Wesley R. Burr, "Satisfactions with Various Aspects of
   Marriage Over the Life Cycle: A Random Middle
   Class Sample," Journal of Marriage and the Family,
   Vol. 32, No. 1, February 1970, pp. 29-37.

8. Ludwig L. Geismar, Preventive Intervention in Social
   Work, Metuchen, N. J. : Scarecrow Press, 1969,
   pp. 58-68.

9. For a discussion of the application of the prevention
   concept of social work see Geismar, Preventive
   Intervention in Social Work, pp. 11-24.

10. Alfred J. Kahn et al. , Neighborhood Information Cen-
     ters, A Study and Some Proposals, New York:
     Columbia University School of Social Work, 1966,
     pp. 46-59.

11. Ibid. , p. 61.

12. Mildred Zucker, "Citizens' Advice Bureaus: The Bri-
     tish Way," Social Work, Vol. 10, No. 4, October
     1965, pp. 85-91.

13. Richard A. Cloward and Irwin Epstein, "Private Social
     Welfare's Disengagement from the Poor: The Case
     of Family Adjustment Agencies," in Mayor N. Zald
     (ed.), Social Welfare Institutions, New York: John
     Wiley, 1965, pp. 623-644.
          Findings from a national service census of the
     Family Service Association of America indicate that
     different social classes have been served more or
     less in proportion to their share in the total popu-
     lation. There is little comfort in this observation
     since it is a well known fact that the lower classes
     have a disproportionate need for services. Dorothy
     Fahs Beck, Patterns in Use of Family Agency Ser-
     vice, New York: Family Service Association of
     America, 1962, pp. 9-11; 36.

14. Alfred J. Kahn, "Therapy, Prevention and Developmen-
     tal Provisions" in Public Health Concepts in Social
     Work Education, New York: Council on Social Work
     Education, 1962, pp. 132-148.

15. Neighborhood centers in the United States "typically pro-
     vide outreach service and otherwise encourage
     agency-shy persons to use the center," write
     O'Donnell and Sullivan. Edward J. O'Donnell and
     Marilyn M. Sullivan, "Service Delivery and Social
     Action Through the Neighborhood Center: A Review
     of Research," Welfare in Review, Vol. 7, No. 6,
     Nov. -Dec. 1969, pp. 1-12, p. 4.

16. George P. Rowe, "The Developmental Conceptual
     Framework to the Study of the Family," in F. Ivan
     Nye and Felix M. Berardo (ed.), Emerging Con-
     ceptual Frameworks in Family Analysis, New York:
     Macmillan, 1966, pp. 198-222.

17. Pitrim Sorokin, Carle C. Zimmerman, and C. J. Galpin, A Systematic Sourcebook in Rural Sociology, Vol. II, Minneapolis: University of Minnesota Press, 1931, p. 31.

18. Roy H. Rodgers, "Toward A Theory of Family Development," Journal of Marriage and the Family, Vol. 26, No. 3, August 1964, pp. 262-270.

19. Evelyn M. Duvall, Family Development, Philadelphia: J. B. Lippincott, 1957, p. 8.

20. Alice S. Rossi, "Transition to Parenthood," in Jeffrey K. Hadden and Marie L. Borgatta (eds.), Marriage and the Family, A Comprehensive Reader, Ithaca, Ill.: F. E. Peacock, 1969, pp. 361-376.

21. E. E. LeMasters, "Parenthood as Crisis," in Marvin B. Sussman (ed.), Sourcebook in Marriage and the Family, Boston: Houghton Mifflin, 1963, pp. 194-198.

22. Arthur P. Jacoby, "Transition to Parenthood: A Reassessment," Journal of Marriage and the Family, Vol. 31, No. 4, November 1969, pp. 720-727.

23. Harold Feldman found that couples rate the first year with the infant as more satisfying than subsequent stages in the family life cycle. Harold Feldman, op. cit. p. 21-22.

24. Alice S. Rossi. loc. cit., p. 372.

25. Ibid., p. 372.

26. Geismar, Preventive Intervention in Social Work,

27. Duvall describes stage IV as families with school children (oldest child 6-13 years) and stage V families as those with teenagers (oldest child 13-20 years). Evelyn M. Duvall, op. cit., p. 8. In the above cited study we had selected families with at least one child in sixth grade of the local middle school. Depending on the number and age of his siblings--if any--the family of these children was likely to fall either into stage IV or V of the Duvall scheme.

Chapter 2

THE STUDY DESIGN AND ITS RATIONALE

There are no shortcuts to testing the validity of propositions concerning the utility of social work practice. The
road to validation is paved with the building blocks of empirical research which include design, sampling, and measurement. They are the alternatives to practice wisdom, intuitive validation, fads and fashions in service rendering, and
other time honored ways of evaluating a professional program.
In order to test whether a program of services, considered
appropriate for the proposed study population, achieves its
objectives it is necessary to develop a design which permits
a comparison of recipients with non-recipients. Such a comparison of population groups must be carried out with reference to a special variable or groups of variables such as
certain types of behavior, attitudes, or functioning; that is,
the factors to be affected by the program of intervention and
measured by the researcher. Before undertaking to review
the experimental design and the process of measurement, it
is necessary to present the rationale for the so-called independent variable of the study, the program of intervention,
which determines to a large extent the nature of the other
facets of the research effort.

The program of intervention of the Family Life Improvement Project (FLIP) was predicated upon the proposition
that professional intervention by social workers can have a
positive effect upon the social functioning of young families.
The term "positive effect" is to be interpreted broadly to
mean more salutary than would be the case without professional services. Thus, positive effect may mean improve-
ment--compared to the situation before services were ren-
dered--or no change or deterioration in functioning. But
whatever the change pattern in the treatment families, it is
postulated to be more positive than in a matched group of
untreated families.

If the hypothesis of the first chapter is borne out by
the longitudinal study and young families do indeed show a

16

trend toward increasing social malfunctioning, positive outcome in the treatment group may well be in the form of un-
changed social functioning or lesser deterioration than in the
untreated group.

There is a special reason for emphasizing the issue
of relative rather than absolute improvement. Professional
intervention is not to be thought of as affecting comprehensive
changes in the life pattern and situation of the families served. More realistically, the proposed services of the Family
Life Improvement Project are designed to meet a developmental need by helping the families adjust to changing situations arising from the social, psychological, and economic
changes occurring during the early part of the family life
cycle. Services are also designed to play a remedial function wherever the family encounters problems in intrapersonal,
interpersonal, or environmental relationships or situations.

The Family Life Improvement Project as conceived
was characterized by what Herbert Aptekar has called the
Gestalt approach to social work. [1] This approach seeks to
bring about changes in individuals, families, small groups,
and the more immediate environment in which the client
resides. According to Aptekar this contrasts with the total-
istic approach which is satisfied with nothing less than major
institutional change. [2] Advocates of the latter, who have become numerous in social work in recent years, tend to believe that comprehensive institutional change is bound to
bring in its wake changes in the small social systems which
include the individual and the family. Those deciding in
favor of the Gestalt approach do not deny that institutional
change affects smaller systems, but they seriously question
whether totalism is the answer to all the problems at the
small systems level. Except for some of the traditionalists
among the Gestalt group who might view behavior change as
the answer to man's problems, supporters of the Gestalt
approach are likely to stress the need for carrying on intervention efforts at both the micro- and the macro-level of
society.

The architects of FLIP never contemplated a program
of action aimed at basic institutional change. Early efforts
aimed at involving the local municipal authorities in planning
met with considerable resistance and had to be abandoned.
It was clear to the directors of FLIP that community collaboration could be attained only at the agency level where exe-
cutives, supervisors, and practitioners might respond

favorably to the idea of a university-based experimental project.   It was equally clear that when bringing the resources
of the community to bear on Project clients, Project roles
would include negotiating, interceding, and playing advocate
on behalf of FLIP families rather than taking action to bring
about changes in community structure and policy.   In spite
of the circumscribed character of this program of intervention, there seemed to be little doubt in the minds of the
Project planners about the need for action research to test
the efficacy of professional intervention.

        This issue of testing the effectiveness of professional
services needs to be viewed within the context of experimental-
control research in which the objectives of intervention have
been clearly defined and outcome has been measured in keeping with these objectives by a reliable and valid instrument.
The field of social work is long on practice experience and
short on objective evidence testifying to the effectiveness of
professional intervention.   In the area of professional service
to families in particular, only a small handful of studies have
been executed which furnish sufficiently reliable techniques of
assessment and controls to permit the drawing of conclusions
relative to outcome.

        Eight studies devoted to assessing the effects of vari-
ous kinds of social work intervention on poor and/or problematic families should be mentioned as meeting the above
criteria.   They are the Franklin County, Ohio Public Welfare
Project;   the New Haven Neighborhood Improvement Project;
the Chemung County Research Demonstration Project with
Multi-Problem Families;   the Vancouver B. C. Area Development Project;   the Community Service Society-Department
of Social Service Study;   the Copenhagen Family Center Project;   the Chicago Midway Study;   and the Delaware Rehabilitation of Dependent Families Project. [3]   This is not an exhaustive list since some well conceived and well executed
projects have not yet shared their findings with readers of
American professional publications.

        Contrary to the impression that social work is an in-
effective means of professional helping, gained after the
publication of Girls at Vocational High[4] and the Chemung
County Study[5], the eight studies cited above reveal different
types of results which range from success to failure if judged
in terms of the goals of the principal investigator.   Though
strongly at odds with the simple notion that casework is not
useful, their cumulative evidence does not add up to support

of the opposite proposition, that casework is necessarily useful or effective, either. It should be noted that these studies
are not naturally cumulative in the sense of employing a common, independent variable whose relationship to a series of
related dependent variables can be examined. They do share
in common the concept of professional intervention, but its
nature differed from study to study. Dependent variable
measurement, interestingly enough, varied less, in that
groups of two and three programs--with two exceptions--
utilized the same instruments for assessing results. Populations, however, differed considerably in age, ethnic composition, economic status, and other factors.

While the variability in the study dimensions makes
comparisons difficult, it is, nonetheless, possible to examine
outcomes relative to type of service rendered and population
served in what remains, after all, a beginning attempt to
view professional intervention from a more rigorous evaluative perspective than that which prevails in the profession.
We shall defer the review and comparison of the above studies until the last chapter when it will be possible to enlarge
the research pool by including the results of the Family Life
Improvement Project. For the present, however, the notion,
derived from a review of earlier outcome studies, that professional social work may lead to the attainment of service
objectives supplies a sufficient rationale for continuing efforts to test the results of professional intervention.

The kind of professional intervention offered in the
Family Life Improvement Project represents a departure
from the traditional concept of rendering service on the
basis of agency competence and specialization. Ordinarily,
a social agency will accept clients whose problems or needs
are congruent with the type of service it offers. Those who
do not need these specific kinds of services are turned away
or referred elsewhere.

In contrast, the Family Life Improvement Project
set for itself the task of responding to any and all kinds of
family need. This was necessary because the Project selected its clientele randomly, naturally precluding exclusion
for reasons of nonsuitability. Acceptance for service, of
course, must not be mistaken for ability to render all kinds
of service. FLIP was designed to address itself to psycho-
social needs in the broadest sense but it did not render
medical treatment, formal education, vocational counseling,
financial assistance, or other specialized services. FLIP's

responsibility, however, extended to helping families obtain specialized services when needed, and that help often included guiding clients through a bureaucratic maze and locating financial resources that made such use possible.

As Project services were not specified a priori but developed and operated in accordance with client need, it was difficult to lay out a blueprint of helping activities before the work got under way. Yet, it seemed unreasonable to start the service program on a purely pragmatic basis without a design outlining types and frequency of worker activity in relation to anticipated client need.

A study completed prior to the start of the Family Life Improvement Project had as goals (1) an assessment of family needs at the time of the arrival of the first child and (2) the construction of a tentative model of services. [6] The study which, like the Family Life Improvement Project, utilized a randomly selected sample of young urban families employed a two-fold approach to model building: (1) a cross-sectional analysis of the social functioning of these families and (2) the extrapolation of developmental change patterns based on a comparison of the cross-sectional functioning patterns of families at the start of the family life-cycle and families some 12 years older. [7]

This two-fold analysis led to an intervention model which differentiated among three levels of problemicity in family functioning and the types of need the families manifested, with special reference to needs in instrumental versus interpersonal and intrapersonal behavior areas. [8] Intervention into problematic situations was seen as putting greater stress on remedial types of services than intervention into situations reflecting adequate or near adequate social functioning. Professional helping in families characterized by the latter type of functioning was more in the nature of educational and developmental work designed to help the family anticipate and plan for future need and explore new ways of gaining satisfactions. This subject is discussed in greater detail in Chapter 7.

The model of intervention referred to here is highly generalized and suggests broad strategies for helping families rather than techniques of service. Social work, particularly social casework, has made the identification and teaching of intervention techniques a central concern of professional practice but the work of Florence Hollis stands out as a unique effort, for it attempts to systematically study these techniques.[9] The Hollis treatment typology did not, however, supply us with a usable scheme for building a treatment model for two reasons: (1) the point of departure of the typology is worker activity rather than, as in our case, client problems; (2) the scheme focuses heavily on verbal interaction between client and worker. By contrast, we anticipated that FLIP social workers would be engaged in a variety of activities other than verbal exchanges with their clients, and these activities would have to come under the purview of systematic data collection and analysis.

In addition to the absence of existing models which relate interventive techniques to client problems, a further condition underscored the necessity for model building. There are very few attempts in professional social work--or for that matter in the fields of counseling and psychotherapy-- to establish blueprints for intervention in the interpersonal situations of normal, young families. One need not even narrow the field of investigation as much as we had done here and still state with some conviction that prevention-focused helping practice, though it has produced some impressive diagnostic models,[10] has generally stopped short of setting up designs for treatment or service.

It is for this reason that the Project undertook to develop some broad guidelines for treatment techniques going beyond the foregoing generalized model of intervention. Once a family was identified as a client or treatment case (not a member of the control group), the assigned social worker would arrange a visit and communicate to the mother that they had been selected to participate in the service program. If the family agreed to cooperate, and few failed to do so, the first task of the worker was to assess the family situation relative to the need for, as well as the nature and frequency of, service. Since all families in the study, including those in the treatment group, had already undergone a two- to three-hour interview and attitude testing during the year prior to the start of the action program, the social worker had to determine in the course of the first treatment contact whether there had occurred any changes since then in the family's social functioning. A decision on the course of the treatment plan was made jointly by the worker and treatment supervisor after studying interview and attitudinal data on the client.

The assessment took into account level of social functioning, types of problems identified, and the family's own
interest in taking advantage of the service offered. Whereas
services to the families as a whole were focused on developmental aspects of family living such as family goals, educational and vocational planning, and the socialization of children, many families presented problems which had to be dealt
with immediately. Well functioning families with no urgent
problems were seen infrequently but no less than four times
a year. Families presenting pressing problems were visited
as often as necessary; this could be as little as once a
month or as much as twice weekly, depending upon the kind
of help needed.

The Family Life Improvement Project presented itself
to its clients as a service that could supply information, advice, guidance, and counseling on matters pertaining to family life and could be helpful in effecting referral to relevant
community resources. The Project saw its role as extending
beyond referral, as playing a negotiating or advocacy role
when the client was unlikely to receive the service to which
he appeared entitled.

The stance of the FLIP worker was invariably one of
reaching-out, since that was the only way to develop a treatment partnership with families who were neither under an
obligation to accept services nor felt pressured by problems--
there were some exceptions--to seek treatment. Difficulties,
even serious ones, were found to exist in some cases, but
problematic families, like American families in general, preferred to rely on their own resources or sought the help of
relatives, friends, and clergymen before resorting to professional assistance.

With problem-ridden families or families expressing
deep concern over specific unmet needs, the worker used a
problem-focused approach from the beginning, not dissimilar
to that used by many family service agencies. With normal
families the family life education theme, stressing educational,
cultural, recreational, and general developmental needs, was
introduced during the early contacts. More often than not as
treatment continued, both approaches tended to be employed
with the emphasis shifting from one to the other depending
on the family's overall pattern of social functioning. The
services were guided by the general expectation that after
the first contacts the clients themselves, recognizing the

advantages of the program, would be motivated to take the initiative and call on the worker between scheduled visits whenever the need arose.

The Project designed an intensive program of in-service training for its social workers as a means of (1) becoming familiar with the vast range of family situations not usually encountered in social agencies; (2) evolving a common developmental and educational philosophy to family treatment; (3) learning to give help in coping with problems common to young families, particularly problems in the areas of child rearing and family planning; and (4) getting to know community resources and ways of dealing with the gaps and shortcomings in the local service structure.

Nobody in the Project and few people in this country have had experience in serving clients who had been co-opted, so to speak, into the client role. We knew that in the absence of negative sanctions we would have to produce convincing evidence justifying our intervention into family life. With seriously problematic families, obviously a small minority in any randomly chosen young population, the problems themselves could become the handle for rendering services. With problem-free families or with families who did not perceive any problems, the study approach would have to be stressed, which made the family members partners in an enterprise designed to gather information about family life and family growth. This turned out to be a helpful beginning stance, but there were few families, even adequately functioning families, who after several contacts, did not involve the social worker in their interests or concerns.

The FLIP worker, in contrast to the worker at a typical family agency or mental health center, had instructions to gear his treatment program to the developmental and preventive aspects of family functioning even in situations where the client faced substantial problems of one kind or another. In keeping with generally accepted casework procedure, the worker was asked to start "where the client is" and to give priority to service in terms of the urgency of the problem. Workers were cautioned against operating with any assumptions regarding the inherent importance or appropriateness of one type of service as against another. As a university-based agency the Family Life Improvement Project, unlike other service agencies, was not burdened

by a mandate for rendering specific kinds of services or by
a tradition which assigns an automatic priority to a certain
type of helping, as for instance treatment in interpersonal
as against instrumental types of functioning.

Measurement in this study had to take into account
those aspects of family life which reflected the family's
ability to carry out socially expected tasks and play social
roles which were satisfying to those performing them. The
concept of social functioning of the family--or family functioning in short--widely employed in social work seemed to
be the best indicant of what the research attempted to measure.

The concept of family functioning has been operation-
alized by means of the St. Paul Scale of Family Functioning[11]
and subsequent instrument refinements[12] and will not be discussed here in detail. Briefly, it measures the role performance of family members against criteria of adequacy in
terms of the following four dimensions: (1) whether laws
are violated or observed; (2) whether behavior contributes
or is harmful to the physical, social, and emotional well-
being of family members; (3) whether behavior is in har-
mony or conflict with the standards of a family's status
group; and (4) whether a family member's behavior is personally satisfying and commensurate with his potential for
social functioning. [13] The social functioning of a family is,
in fact, measured in nine areas and 27 sub-categories on a
continuum of scores ranging from 7, or adequate social
functioning, to 1, or inadequate social functioning, with 4,
or marginal functioning, occupying a middle position.

A sample of 555 young Newark families[14] constituted
the research population. They were selected randomly from
a universe of 3,585 families which were in the register of
first births to mothers under the age of 30 during the year
1964 and the first four months of 1965.[15] The sample was
randomly divided into an experimental group and a control
group of 272 and 283 families, respectively, with the experimental-group families receiving services geared to their
specific levels of social functioning. At the end of the treatment phase or after the third year of treatment, the active
study group had been reduced from 555 to 352, with 177 remaining in the experimental group and 175 in the control
group. Two main factors accounted for the attrition: the
moving of families out of the area and the desire on the
part of the families to terminate participation in the study.

It is of interest that attrition rates in both groups, treatment and control, were similar, 35% and 38%, respectively. [16]

The data reported in Chapter 6, Changes in Family Functioning Related to the Program of Services, is based on the total 352 treatment- and control-group families who remained in the sample through the completion of the treatment phase. In Chapter 7, Patterns of Professional Intervention, the analysis is restricted to the 177 families in the treatment group who continued in the study.

How were the families chosen? The original universe of 3,585 primiparae was secured from the Newark Bureau of Vital Statistics in the Department of Health and Welfare. From them a 50% random sample of 1,800 families was picked to be interviewed. Attempts were made to contact and interview only 1,453 cases, which means that 347 families were left as a sample pool residue, not to be included in the study after enough families had been found for the experimental and control groups.

How did the 1,453 cases shrink to a working group of 555? Although considerable effort was expended in locating respondents, we failed to find as many as 585, or 40%, of the original sample. We were successful in establishing contact with 868. Of the latter, a full 255 families were disqualified since, in one way or another, they failed to meet the criteria for inclusion in the sample. Because 147 out-of-wedlock mothers had placed their children for adoption there was no family to study since adoption procedures preclude inquiries linking the placement to the natural mother. Another 67 mothers had left the area shortly after the birth; 27 more had older children who were not recorded in the birth register; in 14 additional cases infants had died. Of the remaining 613 cases, 58, or 9.5%, refused to be interviewed, bringing the total working sample to 555 families.

The design had stipulated that control-group cases would be interviewed at varying intervals in order to examine a possible effect of interview frequency on measurement over the course of the study. Accordingly, one-sixth, or 45 families, would be seen three times each year; another sixth, or 45 cases, were to be seen twice a year; one-half, or 143, once a year; and one-sixth, or 50, at the beginning and at the end of the project only. [17]

At the termination of the Project the control cases
showed the following attrition rates:[18]

Frequency of Interviews	% Attrition
Three times a year	18%
Twice a year	33%
Once a year	44%
Before and after	26%

These data suggest that control families seen more
often were retained at a somewhat higher rate than those
visited less frequently. However, the relationship does not
hold for "before and after" control cases. A statistical test
(chi square) shows that the relationship between attrition
rates and frequency of contacts is not significant, and that
chance factors are likely to account for the variations noted
above.

The most serious problem in the sampling procedure
arose from the fact that 585, or 49%, of the 1,198 potentially usable research subjects in the study sample could not
be located in spite of our most energetic efforts. This has
considerable implications for sample representativeness,
although, while desirable, it is perhaps of secondary importance in this particular study which was concerned primarily
with the effects of a set of orientations and activities (in this
case a program of intervention) upon the lives of a sample
of young families and not with generalizing from the findings
of the study sample to all young families in the city of
Newark. It should be noted that the investigators did carry
out a special sample validation study, summarized in Appendix B, because of this problem.

Experiment and control groups were studied with the
aid of identical instruments of measurement. The five-year
research had as its primary objective an assessment of
changes in social functioning during the early phases of the
family life cycle. The effects of early intervention covering
a three-year period on the social functioning of the families
was determined by repeated measurement and a comparison
of changes between experimental- and control-group families.

Initial research interviews with the 555 study families
were conducted during the last third of 1964 and the first

eight months of 1965. The sample families which were contacted were requested to participate in a five-year study designed to provide information on family development and on
the means families employ to cope with the problems of city
life. Neither families nor interviewers had any knowledge
of which cases would be assigned to the experimental and
which to the control group.

All initial interviews were done with the mother of
the child whose name appeared on the vital statistics register during the sampling period. The interview was based on
the open-ended interview guideline[19] on which the St. Paul
Scale of Family Functioning is based. In addition to the
interview which lasted about two to three hours, each mother
completed a five-item Srole Anomie Scale[20] as well as 10
five-item PARI (Parental Attitude Research Instruments)
Scales[21] which dealt with attitudes on child rearing and family relations. Both scales were self-administered but were
read to the respondent and checked by the interviewer where
the mother was unable to complete it herself. Some thirty
Puerto Rican mothers who knew little or no English were
interviewed by a Spanish speaking interviewer, and completed
Spanish versions of the Anomie and PARI scales.

The narrative data on family functioning referred to
as the Profile of Family Functioning were coded by a team
of four specially trained coders who remained with the Project until the data analysis was completed. Repeated reliability testing became a standard part of their operation (see
Chapter 3 on data reliability and validity).

Following the random assignment of study cases to
experimental and control groups, data collection by means
of the Profile of Family Functioning was continued. However, second and subsequent interviews were shorter than
the first because they focused mainly on changes in social
functioning and omitted past data, particularly on the history
of families of origin and on events leading up to marriage
or pregnancy if no marriage had taken place.

Interviewers of control group families would complete
a family Profile for each contact regardless of whether it
took place every six months or twice in three-and-a-half
years. The social workers serving experimental-group families also completed Profiles on their families, and they did
so to record changes--or the absence of such--for six-month
periods following the first service contact.

Experimental and control families were engaged in two additional data collection efforts, both taking place at the end of the study. One comprised a study of attitudes regarding community needs and problems and preferred courses of action to cope with such problems, to be reported in a future publication; the other was a self-assessment of changes in family functioning based on the response of Project mothers to a series of structured, self-administered questionnaire items. The latter is discussed in Chapter 8. Here, too, the option existed of having the interviewer or social worker fill out the form.

The most extensive kind of data collection in the Project was carried out in relation to the 272 treatment-group families. The data gathered with the aid of a specially designed Treatment Log[22] represented an effort to document all service activities whether these took place in the home of the client, the FLIP office, or at a social agency or community resource serving the client family. The Treatment Log is a semi-structured schedule which social workers completed for each week of service and which constitutes a record of place and nature of contact (in-person, phone, etc.) with client or collateral, subjects discussed, person who initiated the discussion, and the character of the client-worker exchange (whether aimed at giving or receiving information, direction, or support). Treatment Log data were coded[23] by a separate team of five coders whose major coding effort was concentrated on the reliable identification of method and resources of exchange. In this endeavor, as in the rating of the Profiles, reliability testing was a prerequisite of data collection. All information gathered in this research-action project was transferred to IBM cards and processed by an IBM 360-67 computer.

In characterizing the research one might say that the Project sought to combine the social functioning approach, applied longitudinally over the first five-year span of the family life cycle, with services aimed at early intervention, and if these services proved feasible, they could be interpreted as preventive intervention. The latter concept, borrowed from public health, is used here to denote intervention in a population which has not yet manifested signs of serious malfunctioning but for which it is possible to make statistical predictions about its occurrence if no attempt is made to intervene. The projected study attempted to answer three basic questions: Which families in society tend to

become disorganized? What is the nature of the disorganization process? And how useful is social work in preventing
severe family disorganization?

The research approach was both epidemiological[24] and
longitudinal. The Project undertook to study the prevalence
and incidence of family disorganization among young families
with the aid of a representative, community-wide sample.
Instead of relying upon retrospective data as was done in an
earlier study,[25] data collection on family functioning was
carried out by means of interviews and observations covering
the families' patterns of behavior in the present.

The significance of preventive intervention must be
seen within the context of the basic character of service to
families in trouble in the United States. At the risk of
oversimplifying a complex situation we, nonetheless, believe
that the following characterization is essentially accurate:
services tend to be remedial rather than preventive.[26] They
greatly favor the motivated over the non-motivated client.
Moreover, the highly specialized and institutionalized social
service structure in the United States becomes a major determinant in service giving, with the result that established
service patterns rather than client need often shape the nature of professional intervention.[28] In the Family Life Improvement Project we attempted to respond to all kinds of
need as they arose and to help with anticipated developmental
stresses, striving to act as a truly preventive intervenor.

Notes

1. Herbert Aptekar, "Social Work in a Complex Society,
    Its Utility and Effectiveness," paper presented at the
    Pacific Southwest Regional Institute, San Diego, Cali-
    fornia, October 1969 (unpublished).

2. Ibid., p. 5.

3. The corresponding publications reporting the findings
    are: John H. Behling, An Experimental Study to
    Measure the Effectiveness of Casework Services,
    Columbus, Ohio: Franklin County Welfare Depart-
    ment, 1961 (mimeographed Ph.D. Dissertation, Ohio
    State University, 1961). L. L. Geismar and Jane
    Krisberg, The Forgotten Neighborhood, Metuchen,

N. J. : Scarecrow Press, 1967, pp. 318-358. Gordon Brown (ed.), The Multi-Problem Dilemma, Metuchen, N. J. : Scarecrow Press, 1968. L. I. Bell and Gillian Wilder, "Family Functioning in Multi-Problem Families," in The Area Development Project, Research Monograph III. Vancouver, B. C. : Area Development Project 1969 (mimeographed), pp. 60-86. Edward J. Mullen, Robert M. Chazin, and David M. Feldstein, Preventing Chronic Dependency, New York: Community Service Society, 1970 (mimeographed). P. H. Kühl, The Family Center Project - Action Research on Socially Deprived Families, Copenhagen: The Danish National Institute of Social Research, 1969. Edward E. Schwartz and William C. Sample, "First Findings from Midway," Social Service Review, Vol. 41, No. 2, June 1967, pp. 113-151. Robert A. Wilson, "An Evaluation of Intensive Casework Impact," Public Welfare, October 1967, pp. 301-306. Community Services Council of Delaware, Evaluation of Pilot Project in the Rehabilitation of Dependent Families, Wilmington, Del. : May 1966 (mimeographed).

4. Henry J. Meyer, Edgar P. Borgatta, and Wyatt C. Jones, Girls at Vocational High, New York: Russell Sage Foundation, 1965.

5. Gordon E. Brown, op. cit.

6. Geismar, Preventive Intervention in Social Work; for an abbreviated statement on the proposed program see L. L. Geismar and Jane Krisberg, "The Family Life Improvement Project: An Experiment in Preventive Intervention," Social Casework, Part I, Vol. 47, No. 9, November 1966, pp. 563-70; Part II, Vol. 47, No. 10, December 1966, pp. 663-667.

7. Ibid. , pp. 58-70.

8. Ibid. , pp. 70-81.

9. Florence Hollis, Casework, A Psychosocial Therapy, New York: Random House, 1964. Florence Hollis, Development of a Casework Treatment Typology, Final Report to the National Institute of Mental Health, New York: Columbia University School of Social Work, 1966 (mimeographed).

10.   An outstanding example of this is the Stirling County
       Study of Psychiatric Disorder and Sociocultural En-
       vironment.   See especially Volume 2, Charles C.
       Hughes, Marc-Adelard Tremblay, et al. , People of
       Cove and Woodlot, New York: Basic Books, 1960;
       and Volume 3, Dorothea C. Leighton, John S. Hard-
       ing, et al. , The Character of Danger, New York:
       Basic Books, 1963.

11.   L. L. Geismar and Beverly Ayres, Measuring Family
       Functioning, A Manual on a Method for Evaluating
       the Social Functioning of Disorganized Families, St.
       Paul,. Minn. :   Family Centered Project, 1960; L. L.
       Geismar and Michael E. LaSorte, Understanding the
       Multi-Problem Family, A Conceptual Analysis and
       Exploration in Early Identification, New York: Asso-
       ciation Press, 1964.

12.   L. L. Geismar, Michael A. LaSorte, and Beverly Ayres,
       "Measuring Family Disorganization," Marriage and
       Family Living, Vol. 24, No. 1, February 1962, pp.
       51-56;   L. L. Geismar, "Family Functioning as an
       Index of Need for Welfare Services," Family Process,
       Vol. 3, No. 1, March 1964, pp. 99-113.   The most
       comprehensive data on reliability of the St. Paul Scale
       of Family Functioning were recently made available as
       part of an evaluative study conducted by Dr. David Wal-
       lace of Columbia University.   In this research he em-
       ployed both inter-rater reliability as well as indepen-
       dent team ratings to establish scale reliability.   In addi-
       tion, he compared ratings of the St. Paul Scale with
       those obtained by using the Hunt-Kogan Movement Scale.
       See Gordon E. Brown, op. cit. , pp. 107-181.   See also
       David Wallace, "Chemung County Evaluation of Case-
       work Services to Dependent Multi-Problem Families,"
       The Social Service Review, Vol. 41, No. 4, December
       1967, pp. 379-389.   See also the revised version of the
       manual on measurement by L. L. Geismar, Family and
       Community Functioning, Metuchen, N. J. :   Scarecrow
       Press, 1971.

13.   L. L. Geismar, "Family Functioning as an Index of
       Need for Welfare Services," loc. cit. , p. 101.

14.   The original sample comprised 855 cases including 300
       families in an after-only group which was to supply
       indications of a control effect due to interviewing.

The high attrition rate of the after-only group--only
82 families could be located--and the delay in obtaining these interviews made this group useless for the
study.

15. Because of a heavy attrition rate the universe from
     which the sample was drawn had to be enlarged.
     This was done by lengthening from 8 to 16 months
     the time period during which first births to mothers
     under 30 were reported.

16. Tables 1 - 4 in Appendix A show that at the outset of
     the study, despite attrition, the experimental and
     control groups were essentially alike with regard to
     the major dependent variable, social functioning, and
     selected demographic characteristics.

17. The original N's called for by the design were 50, 50,
     150, and 50. The smaller number of cases that
     actually materialized in each category reflects first
     stage attrition of various kinds.

18. For details on the nature and timing of the attrition,
     see Ludwig L. Geismar, Ursula Gerhart, and Bruce
     Lagay, in collaboration with Harriet Fink and Isabel
     Wolock, The Rutgers University Family Life Improve-
     ment Project - Final Report (Preliminary Version),
     New Brunswick, N. J.: Rutgers University Graduate
     School of Social Work, February 1970, pp. 10-28.

19. Ludwig L. Geismar, Family and Community Functioning,
     Metuchen, N. J.: Scarecrow Press, 1971.

20. Leo Srole, "Social Integration and Certain Corollaries:
     An Exploratory Study," American Sociological Re-
     view, Vol. XXI, No. 6, December 1956, pp. 709-716.
     Findings derived from the use of this and the PARI
     scales will be reported in a forthcoming publication.

21. Earl S. Schaefer and Richard Q. Bell, "Development of
     a Parental Attitude Research Instrument," Child
     Development, Vol. XXIX, No. 3, September 1958,
     pp. 339-361.

22. For a description of the Log and the method of docu-
     menting services see Bruce Lagay and L. L. Geis-
     mar, The Treatment Log - A Recording Procedure

for Casework Practice and Research, New Brunswick, N. J.: Graduate School of Social Work, Rutgers University (mimeographed).

23. For details of the procedure see Bruce Lagay, A Manual on a Method for Coding Worker-Client Activity in Social Casework, New Brunswick, N. J.: Graduate School of Social Work, Rutgers University, 1969 (mimeographed).
                                                          o
24. Brian McMahon, et al., Epidemiological Methods, Boston: Little, Brown, 1960; Hugh R. Leavell and E. G. Clark, Preventive Medicine for the Doctor in his Community, New York: McGraw Hill, 1958; Wilson G. Smillie, Preventive Medicine and Public Health, 2nd ed., New York: Macmillan, 1955; Dorothea C. Leighton, John S. Harding, et al., The Character of Danger, New York: Basic Books, 1963, pp. 13-29.

25. L. L. Geismar and Michael A. LaSorte, "Factors Related to Family Disorganization," Marriage and Family Living, Vol. 24, No. 4, November 1963, pp. 479-481.

26. Milton Wittman, "Preventive Social Work: A Goal for Practice and Education," Social Work, Vol. 6, No. 1, January 1961, pp. 19-28; Bertram Beck, "Can Social Work Prevent Social Problems?" Social Welfare Forum, 1960, pp. 180-193; Lydia Rapoport, "Working with Families in Crisis: An Exploration in Preventive Intervention," Social Work, Vol. 7, No. 3, July 1962, pp. 48-56; Berta Fantl, "Preventive Intervention," Social Work, Vol. 7, No. 3, July 1962, pp. 41-47; Council on Social Work Education, Concepts of Prevention and Control: Their Use in the Social Work Curriculum, New York, 1961; Florence E. Cyr and Shirley H. Wathenberg, "Social Work in the Preventive Program of Maternal and Child Health," Social Work, Vol. 2, No. 3, July 1957, pp. 32-38.

27. Richard A. Cloward and Irwin Epstein, op. cit.; See also the findings which highlight obstacles to provision of adequate casework service to the lower classes in Dorothy Fahs Beck, op. cit.

28.   Harold L. Wilensky and Charles N. Lebeaux, Industrial Society and Social Welfare, New York: Russell Sage Foundation, 1958, Chapter X, pp. 233-282; David Landy, "Problems of a Person Seeking Help in our Culture," Social Welfare Forum 1960, New York: Columbia University Press, 1960, pp. 127-245; S. Kirson Weinberg, "Social Action Systems and Social Problems," Arnold Rose (ed.), Human Behavior and Social Process, Boston: Houghton Mifflin, 1962, pp. 401-424; Alvin W. Gouldner, "The Secrets of Organization," Social Welfare Forum 1963, New York: Columbia University Press, 1963, pp. 166-177.

Chapter 3

DATA RELIABILITY AND VALIDITY

The key measurements of this study hinge on the use of the concept family functioning. We therefore considered it necessary to examine the reliability and validity of this major dependent variable. Fortunately, several previous studies had addressed themselves to these issues, particularly the St. Paul and New Haven studies which provided tests of scale reliability[1] and the Chemung County Research in which both scale reliability and validity were scrutinized. [2]

In using the St. Paul Scale of Family Functioning in the present study, we followed our customary procedure of carrying out additional tests of reliability and validity instead of relying upon the findings of earlier studies. This more conservative approach is recommended whenever, as was the case here, new teams of coders are being employed or the study population is different from that of previous studies in which methodological tests were undertaken.

The study sample of the Family Life Improvement Project is less problematic in social functioning than those used in the studies cited above. This characteristic expressed itself in a skewed score distribution and a smaller variance than was found in previous studies. A testing of the relationship between variance and inter-rater agreement showed the two to be negatively and significantly associated, meaning that high reliability is partly a function of limited score distribution. This finding curtailed efforts to determine the reliability and validity of the instrument by using the standard technique of ordinal measurement. Instead, we devised a new approach for reliability and validity testing, relying largely on nominal measures.

Briefly, the procedure entailed an investigation of a sub-sample of families, comparing the extent of correspondence between information about family life provided by the mother (the primary source of data for the study) and information procured from a second family member, the father.

This general approach to assessing validity by looking at the correspondence between the reports of two persons about the same event or situation has been employed by a number of social scientists.   A brief and selective review of the literature revealed, for the most part, a high degree of agreement between self reports and the reports of others, or external information sources, in subject areas that were of central importance in this study. [3]

Initially, we had planned to interview a random sample of 40 husbands and wives, drawn from the 377 two-parent families included in our active sample.   The very nature of this investigation dictated that only two-parent families could be included, and this eliminated about a third of the cases—those headed by a single parent who was unmarried, separated, or divorced.   Once the sample of 40 cases was drawn, a major difficulty presented itself.   It was much more difficult to arrange interviews with husbands from problem families than with husbands from more adequately functioning families.   Repeated substitutions had to be made for husbands who could not be reached, and therefore the sub-sample differed substantially from the universe of families.   Twenty-five percent of the cases in the sub-sample were rated as totally adequate against a 12% rate in the study sample as a whole.   Furthermore, comparing the sub-sample with the total Project population, it can be seen that Negroes, Protestants, and lower-class families are underrepresented (see Table 1).   Other demographic characteristics of the two groups are also shown in this table.   In short, the 40 cases included in this sub-study represent a group of relatively stable, urban families at the beginning of the family life cycle.

Data procured from the men were based on a single interview lasting approximately two hours.   Their wives had been participating in the Family Life Improvement Project, either as members of a treatment or control group, for the past two years.   In order to get from both husband and wife a picture of family functioning reflecting the same period, the interview with the husband was scheduled as closely as possible to the re-interview with the wife.   However, since interviewers found it difficult to find a time when husbands could be seen privately, an average of four weeks elapsed between respective appointments.

Two kinds of measurement were undertaken to assess the degree of agreement between husbands and wives.   In

Table 1

Comparison on Selected Demographic Variables
of Validity Study Sample and Total Study Population*

Validity Study Sample	(N = 40)		Total Study Population (N= 555)	
	No.	%	No.	%
Negro	15	37. 5	338	60. 9
White	25	62. 5	192	34. 6
Catholic	17	42. 5	185	33. 8
Protestant	15	37. 5	316	57. 7
Jewish	5	12. 5	15	2. 7
Mixed Religions	3	7. 5	28	5. 1
Social Status[†] I & II	3	7. 5	16	3. 0
III	6	15. 0	27	5. 0
IV	3	7. 5	55	10. 2
V	21	52. 5	241	44. 6
VI	7	17. 5	201	37. 2
No. of children, at end of study				
One	17	42. 5	263	47. 6
Two	19	47. 5	208	37. 7
Three	4	10. 0	67	12. 1
Four plus	0	0	14	2. 6

*Numbers in the category groups of the study population do not necessarily add up to 555 or percentages to 100 because of the omission of residual groupings not represented in the study sample or because information on some variables was missing.

[†]Social status groupings are based on the William Wells' adaptation of the Hollingshead two-factor Index of Social Position. William Wells, "The Index of Social Position," Rutgers University, 1962 (unpublished paper).

the first, the St. Paul Scale of Family Functioning was employed and, like the broader study of which this was a part,
the interview data were coded on a seven-point continuum
(see Chapter 2 for details).   This approach had to be abandoned because of the measurement problems inherent in ap-
plying the procedure to a small homogeneous sample.   The
fairly high measure of agreement between husbands and wives
which this method revealed was regarded as deceptive.   On
a category by category basis, about two-thirds of the observations on family functioning were rated as adequate (7)
while 21% were rated as near adequate (6).   Only 12% were
rated above-marginal and below (5 or less).

In order to overcome these problems we devised
another technique for testing the accuracy of interview data.
This compared husband and wife responses not on the normative concept of family functioning but on six discrete dimensions of family life.   The six dimensions were selected
because they were seen to constitute variables that combine
information from all the eight family functioning areas which
had served as the framework for data collection.   At the
same time, these dimensions tapped a variety of categories
of behavior which have no constant relationship--as does
social functioning--to familial adequacy.   Alternatives for
rating each item range from three on the first three variables to a larger but unspecified number--covering nominal
data--on the subsequent three variables.

The six dimensions and a summary of the principal
criteria for coding are given below:

1.   Physical Well-Being of (1)Husband, (2)Wife, (3)Child(ren)

   Good   -   Absence of serious or frequent illness or
                  chronic condition;   absence of physical
                  handicaps of a disabling nature.

   Fair   -   Mild chronic illness or physical handicap
                  present, not hindering a person's daily
                  functioning.

   Poor   -   Serious or frequent illness;   chronic con-
                  dition or serious physical handicap which
                  prevents effective functioning.

2. Emotional Well-Being of (1)Husband, (2)Wife, (3)Child(ren)

   Good   -   Adjustment to environment and ability to
                    form interpersonal relationships is ade-
                    quate; flexible and reality-oriented in
                    interaction with people; has positive self-
                    image; feels able to cope with and suc-
                    ceed in life situations.

   Fair   -   Some problems in adjustment to environ-
                    ment are apparent but not of such a se-
                    vere nature as to cause serious malfunc-
                    tioning; some feelings of inadequacy and
                    insecurity present.

   Poor   -   Poor adjustment to environment; limited
                    ability to form interpersonal relationships;
                    psychosis or extreme neurosis present;
                    feels unable to cope with life situation.

3. Satisfactions (1) Intra-Familial, (2) Extra-Familial,
                  (3) Instrumental, (4) Sexual

   High   -   Pleasure gained from interaction with
                    others and from the performance of tasks
                    within the family and on the outside.

   Medium   -   Limited enjoyment from interacting with
                    others or from the performance of tasks.

   Low   -   General dissatisfaction with interaction in
                    the family and outside the home; lack of
                    satisfaction from the performance of tasks.

4. Role Allocation in (1) Child Rearing, (2) Household Tasks,
                       (3) Financial Management

   The question posed is who carries out what tasks? Are
   they carried out singly by one parent, jointly by both
   parents, allocated to someone outside the family, or
   accomplished by some other arrangement?

5. Goals, Values and Beliefs in the Areas of (1) Education,
                    (2) Priority of Purchases, (3) Religion

   The question to be answered is who believes what?

Do the marriage partners express similar or dissimilar preferences and goals in the three areas designated?

6. Decision Making in (1) Economic Management, (2) Child Rearing, (3) Social and Recreational Activities

Information sought here covers the question who decides what? Regardless of what the parents' wishes and goals may be, who are the people in the family or outside of it who make decisions in the above areas? Are decisions made by one person or are they made jointly?

The 40 sets of interviews with the husbands and wives were rated by two coders each [eight coders worked on this Project] in terms of whether the information supplied by the marriage partners was (1) Identical, i.e., information coincided on each dimension and sub-dimension; (2) Mixed, i.e., some information was similar and some was contradictory; or (3) Contradictory, meaning that the information given by one did not tally with that supplied by the other. Coders carried out independent ratings, and these are the bases for the reliability rates reported here. Mixed and contradictory information was combined into one category and counted as non-agreement responses. The reliability ratio represents the number of observations on which the raters agree, divided by the total number of observations made in each one of the foregoing 19 sub-categories. The six dimensions were divided into three sub-categories each, except for dimension number 3, satisfactions, which contained four sub-categories.

Reliability ratios ranged from a high of .95 for physical well-being of husband to a low of .65 for sexual satisfactions. The mean ratio was .80 with a standard deviation of .068. This denoted fairly satisfactory inter-rater reliability and provided a basis for comparing the response patterns of husbands and wives.

In order to make possible a comparison between husband and wife responses, the 20% of cases upon whose ratings the two coders had not agreed were assigned a single rating at an inter-coder conference. These conference ratings were arrived at after reviewing individual ratings and either eliminating error in one of the ratings or reinterpreting a set of unclear or ambiguous data. The agreement ratios for the protocols by husbands and wives are shown in Table 2. The mean ratio is .80 with a standard deviation of .067.

Table 2

Husband - Wife Agreement on Six
Family Life Variables

Variable	Ratio of Agreement	x^2
Physical Well-being of		
Husband	.80	6.64
Wife	.83	8.06
Child(ren)	.93	15.64
Emotional Well-being of		
Husband	.78	5.40
Wife	.83	8.06
Child(ren)	.75	4.32
Satisfactions		
Intra-Familial	.75	4.32
Extra-Familial	.70	2.56*
Instrumental	.80	6.64
Sexual	.68	1.86*
Role Allocation in		
Child Rearing	.90	9.62
Household Tasks	.90	9.62
Financial Management	.83	8.06
Goals, Values, Beliefs		
Education	.90	9.62
Priority of Purchases	.78	5.40
Religion	.78	5.40
Decision Making		
Economic Management	.73	3.38*
Child Rearing	.78	5.40
Social and Recreational		
Activities	.78	5.40

Mean Ratio = .80; S. D. = .067

*Not significant at the 5% level

Disagreement between husbands and wives on information covered by the six variables appears low to moderate. State of physical well-being and role allocation were reported with a somewhat higher degree of unanimity (mean ratios of .853 and .876 respectively), satisfactions of family members (mean ratio .733) with a somewhat lower degree than the other variables. Observations on the two former are based on more or less objectively verifiable phenomena with a high degree of visibility. [4]

The dimensions labelled satisfactions, decision-making, emotional well-being, and goals, values, beliefs, all of which show a lower ratio of husband-wife agreement, conversely represent variables that are less tangible and more subject to individual interpretation. On the variable sexual satisfactions nearly a third of the couples were in disagreement; lack of agreement here might be seen as a function of the sensitivity of the subject. Evidence from other studies on this subject is not uniform, [5] but we have reason to believe that in the case of our own study the interviewers themselves were hesitant to pose questions and frequently settled for vague, hard-to-code responses. Table 2 shows, nevertheless, that 16 out of 19 agreement ratios were statistically significant at the 5% level or better.

The researchers investigated the hypothesis that husband-wife agreement was significantly correlated with social class. Underlying the formulation of the hypothesis was the following line of reasoning: socially acceptable interview data had been found to be more accurate than data that were less conforming to societal norms. [6] Contrasted to problematic families, adequate families were more apt to give information that coincided with societal norms and, in line with the above finding, that was also likely to be more accurate. Since social class was found to be positively associated with adequacy of family functioning, [7] we expected to also find social class positively correlated with consensus between husband and wife.

The foregoing hypothesis, however, received very little support, for the correlation (gamma) between social status as measured by the modified Hollingshead Index of Social Position (see footnote to Table 1) and degree of agreement between the spouses was +.25 and statistically not significant. Non-support of this hypothesis might be due to two facts: Differences in response patterns were minimized as a result of sample homogeneity, and much of the coded information was of a factual nature, thus less class related than normative data on family functioning.

At first glance it may be argued that in comparing the views of marriage partners we are merely testing the reliability of responses, because we are correlating the independent reports of two informants. But such an interpretation disregards the chief role of the respondents. They are not research aides or participant observers but rather family members who happen to be called upon to describe the family's functioning as they directly experience and perceive it. In other words, in this sub-study we are not seeking to learn whether husband and wife are reliable informers but rather whether what they tell us happens to be true.

Truth in this instance denotes correspondence between verbal reports and what is actually happening in the family. In the absence of data based on direct and unobtrusive observation, we assume that the reports of husband and wife are substantially correlated with the way family members behave, interact, carry out their tasks, and deal with diverse problems. There is the further assumption, which basically justifies the designation "validity study," that high agreement between the independent protocols of husband and wife pairs is an indication that their reporting reflects the actual social functioning of the family.

It may be argued, of course, that high agreement means nothing other than successful collaboration in reporting falsehood. While such an occurrence is always possible, certain controls built into the research process lead one to dismiss the idea of collusion aimed at distortion. In our particular case husbands and wives had little to gain by presenting a contrived story. Moreover, the wives had already been seen and interviewed a number of times prior to the validity test and were not likely to prepare a different version of their views about family life. The men, by contrast, did not know before the interview what kind of information they were expected to furnish and were not likely to come prepared for the occasion.

What statements, if any, can be made about the accuracy of interview data on family functioning? A mean accuracy of 80% and a standard deviation of 6.70% on a comparison of husbands' and wives' responses put the present study in line with some of the more confidence-inspiring findings reported in the literature. Also in line with other studies, higher agreement between the response pairs was generally correlated with concreteness and visibility of information, and lower agreement was associated with subject sensitivity, abstractness, and subjectivity of data. A 20% level of disagreement or inaccuracy does not answer the question of what measure of inaccuracy may be considered acceptable validity. The obvious goal of the researcher is to minimize discrepancies or eliminate them altogether. By extending and refining the few existing propositions on validity into a more coherent theory, guidelines can be developed to help researchers transform the process of data collection from a hit-and-miss operation into a reasonably scientific procedure.

Notes

1. Geismar and Ayres, op. cit. ; Geismar and Krisberg, The Forgotten Neighborhood, pp. 320-321.

2. Brown, op. cit. , pp. 107-189; Wallace, loc. cit.

3. Leonard Weller and Elmer Luchterhand, "Comparing Interviews and Observations on Family Functioning," Journal of Marriage and the Family, 31:1, February 1969, pp. 115-123; Alexander L. Clark and Paul Wallin, "The Accuracy of Husbands' and Wives' Reports of the Frequency of Marital Coitus," Population Studies, 18, November 1964, pp. 165-173; J. Richard Udry and Naomi M. Morris, "A Method for Validation of Sexual Data," Journal of Marriage and the Family, 29:3, August 1967, pp. 442-446; Carol H. Weiss and Allen H. Barton, "Validity of Interview Responses of Welfare Mothers," Research Brief, 2:1, August 15, 1968, Division of Research and Demonstration Grants, Social and Rehabilitation Service, Dept. of Health, Education and Welfare; John R. Clark and Larry L. Tifft, "Polygraph and Interview Validation of Self Reported Deviant Behavior," American Sociological Review, 31:4, August 1966, pp. 516-523; Hugh J. Parry and Helen M. Crossley, "Validity of Responses to Survey Questions," Public Opinion Quarterly, 14, Spring 1950, pp. 61-80.

4. Weller and Luchterhand, <u>loc. cit.</u>

5. Clark and Wallin, <u>loc. cit.</u>, and also Udry and Morris,
    <u>loc. cit.</u>

6. Weiss and Barton, <u>loc. cit.</u>

7. Geismar, <u>Preventive Intervention in Social Work</u>, pp.
    36-43.

Chapter 4

SETTING AND SOCIAL CHARACTERISTICS
OF THE POPULATION

The setting for the study was Newark, New Jersey,
located some ten miles west of the heart of New York City,
with a population of slightly over 400,000 distributed over
23.6 square miles. There were several reasons why Newark
was selected. The emphasis of this research-action project
was upon the urban family and urban services, and Newark
is the largest community in New Jersey, the state where
Rutgers University is located. Its population is large enough
to supply a cohort of 900 primiparae from the records of
one year's registration. (Attrition made it necessary to extend the period to 16 months.) In addition, Newark, which
houses a branch of Rutgers University, was a city where
research space was available in 1964.[1]

According to a Rutgers study done in 1967, Newark
has a household population of 402,000 of which 52.2% are
Negroes, 38.8% white, and 9.5% "others", most of whom
are Spanish speaking of Puerto Rican origin.[2] Newark ranks
second among major U. S. cities (after Washington, D. C.)
in the proportion of black population. It has the largest per
capita public housing program in the nation, sheltering 12%
of the population, and ranks fifth in amount received for
urban renewal. Toward the end of the project period the
city was saturated with community organization programs
designed to reduce unemployment and poverty.

These far-reaching measures notwithstanding, the city
of Newark has all the characteristics of an economically de-
pressed area. Current U. S. population reports list the
median family income for 1967 as $8,017. In Newark, by
contrast, 58% of the families earn less than $7,000 per
year;[3] the corresponding percentage for the U. S. is 41.1.
Nationally, the percentage for those earning under $5,000 is
25.1%; for Newark, 38%. The comparable percentages for
Negroes and whites in the city are 42% and 29%.[4] A third
of city housing is substandard or dilapidated[5] and unemployment affects 9% of the civilian labor force.[6]

46

Although in numbers the Newark household population has remained steady since 1950--the census for that year counted 417,000 persons, the 1960 census 397,000, and the above quoted estimate for 1967 was 402,000[7]--the population composition has changed radically. Between 1950 and 1960, the percentage of Negroes in the city rose from 18% to 34%. The estimate for 1967 is 52%. Puerto Ricans, less than 2.5% of the population in 1960, constituted nearly 10% in 1967. The white population, still a clear majority group in 1960, was estimated to account for no more than 40% of Newark inhabitants in 1967.[8] The Rutgers study also showed that more than 40% of Newark adult Negroes (age 16 and over) had lived there ten years or less, while the comparable figure for "others," mostly Puerto Ricans, was 78% and for whites, only 17.5%.[9] The bulk or 54% of adult resident Puerto Ricans had come to Newark from Puerto Rico, and about a fourth originated in New York, Pennsylvania, and the New England States. Against this, roughly half the whites had always resided in Newark, and another 45% came from other places in New Jersey, the Middle Atlantic and New England States, or abroad. Nearly half of the black adult residents had moved to Newark from Georgia, Alabama, North and South Carolina, and Florida, with other southern states accounting for most of the remaining points of origin. Only 17% of the adult Negroes had always resided in Newark, and less than a fourth had migrated from other New Jersey communities or states outside the American South. Though the Newark pattern of ethnic in-and-out-migration appears similar to that of other American cities, it seems to differ mainly in the pace with which blacks and Puerto Ricans moved into the city.

In short, the city in which this study was carried out is characterized by minority groups, poverty, and rapid population changes. Since the mid-sixties and particularly since the riots in July, 1967, the politics of Newark have been characterized by open confrontation. The New Jersey Governor's Select Commission on Civil Disorder reports "a pervasive feeling of corruption" among Newarkers.[10] The study cites a commission survey which showed that only 21% of Negroes and 19% of whites believed that Newark was presently a good place in which to live.[11] Whites and blacks were quoted as holding divergent views on the causes of the riots.[12]

The data on the social characteristics of the study population of young families are based on the 555 families,

272 treatment and 283 control group cases, which were mentioned in Chapter 2. The reader will remember that the
research design had specified that cases selected for the
study would be primiparae with the mother's age being less
than 30. The presence of the father was not a consideration
in the sample selection, and it was noted that the high rate
of out-of-wedlock births in the universe of primiparae, 43%,
would be reflected in the sample as well. The lower percentage of 31. 0 can be explained largely by placements,
especially of white children, which resulted in a break-up
of the original family. [13] The marital status of the research
population at the beginning of the study was as follows:

Married	67. 1%
Separated	1. 5%
Divorced	. 4%
Out-of-Wedlock	31. 0%
Total (N= 551)	100. 0%

The ethnic make-up of the research population was
as follows: 60. 9% of the families were Negro, 34. 6% white,
4. 1% Puerto Rican[14] and . 4% represented racially mixed
marriages (N= 555).

The religious composition of the families in the study
was 57. 7% Protestant, 33. 8% Catholic, and 2. 7% Jewish.
Protestant-Catholic and Gentile-Jewish marriages characterized 5. 8% of the study population. Information on religion
was missing for 7 families.

The modal age at marriage was between 19 and 20
for the women and between 21 and 22 for the men in the
sample. [15] Negro women, on the average, had married at
a slightly younger age than white women. This is evidenced
in the finding that 39. 2% of Negro women compared with
26. 6% of white women had married by the age of 18. A
similar finding was observed for men, 32. 0% of Negro men
having married by age 20 compared with 23. 0% of white
men. [16]

The low social status of the study population, and by
implication of young Newark families, was reflected in the
occupational distribution of the sample: Families where the
head of the household was unemployed, without an occupation,
or chronically on public assistance constituted 18. 1% and

families headed by unskilled workers another 17.1%.   Families headed by semi-skilled blue collar and service workers
constituted 25.2% of the sample and the skilled blue collar
employee another 20.6% of the study population.   At the
upper-most levels of occupational status were only 19.0% of
the families, headed by persons holding professional, administrative, entrepreneurial and managerial, and other white
collar positions.   The occupational analysis included only
520 families, the balance of 35 cases representing situations
where no husband was present and the mother was completely
financially dependent on her family of origin.

Men and women in this study showed similar educational backgrounds,[17] the modal group in each instance made
up of high school graduates (36.3% of the men and 37.7% of
the women).   Fewer than 5% (3.9% of the men and 4.6% of
the women) of the parents had less than eighth-grade education.   Against this, only 13.4% of the men and 6.6% of the
women went to college, and of these only about a third
graduated with at least a bachelor's degree.

Another index of socio-economic functioning, family
income, yielded further evidence of the families' deprived
social status.   About one-fifth of the families had annual incomes below $3,000, roughly a third had incomes below
$4,000,[18] and nearly two-thirds earned less than $6,000.
The full distribution of family incomes is shown below.

Family Income	% of Families*(N=508)
Under $2,000	13.0
$2,000 - $2,999	6.5
$3,000 - $3,999	13.8
$4,000 - $4,999	14.0
$5,000 - $5,999	17.3
$6,000 - $6,999	9.6
$7,000 - $7,999	7.9
$8,000 - $8,999	4.3
$9,000 - $9,999	1.0
$10,000 - $14,999	4.7
$15,000 and over	.6
Income not computed because family lives as part of another family unit	7.3

*No information on income was available on 47 families.

The income distribution for the study families shows this group was poorer than Newark families as a whole,[19] a difference which can be accounted for by the youth of heads of families. The incomes of Negro families were substantially below those of white families, with 27.6% of the former as against 3.3% of the latter earning under $3,000 a year. The percentages for those who earned less than $6,000 are 70.5% for the Negroes and 52.5% for the whites.

Almost 8% of the families were fully supported by public assistance at the beginning of the study and another 7% received partial support (N=554). Nearly 66% were self-supporting through employment. The balance of the study population was supported by relatives, insurances, part-time employment, or a combination of these. Relatively more Negroes than whites (21.4% and 3.1%) received some form of public assistance, and the proportion of those who were self-supporting by means of employment also differed considerably (52.2% and 88.0%, respectively).

The overall indicant of social status, derived from the Hollingshead Index of Social Position[20] and taking into account the education and occupation of family heads, reveals that 8.0% of the families fell into the top classes I to III, 10.2% fell into Class IV, but 44.6% and 37.2% fell into classes V and VI respectively (N=540). Here, too, Negro-white differences were very pronounced; 2.2% of Negro families against 18.9% of the white families fell into the three top status groups. By contrast, 15.3% of the whites but nearly half (48.3%) of the Negroes were classified as Class VI cases.

Just over one-half of the parents, 53.1% of the mothers and 54.4% of the fathers,[21] were natives of Newark or vicinity. Approximately one-quarter of the parents arrived in Newark before 1960, and another quarter settled there between 1960 and 1964, the beginning of the study. Negroes and whites, however, differed strongly in their residence patterns, with 72.9% of white mothers and 73.1% of white fathers reporting that they were born in or near the city, while only 44.8% of the black mothers and 44.5% of the black fathers listed Newark as their place of birth. Modal migration patterns for those not born in the city were south to north for the Negroes (50.5% of mothers and 40.5% of fathers) and from other parts of the North or from another country for whites (both categories when combined comprise nearly 30% of mothers as well as fathers).

Fifteen percent of white fathers and 10.4% of white mothers
were foreign born, but the latter group constituted less than
one-half percent of the Negro participants in the study. The
Negroes were twice as likely as the whites to have migrated
to Newark from a rural area or a small town.

Notes

1. Ample facilities were made available through the cour-
   tesy of Dr. Leontine Young and the Child Service
   Association.

2. Jack Chernick, Bernard P. Indik, and George Sternlieb,
   Newark, New Jersey, Population and Labor Force,
   New Brunswick, N. J., Rutgers - The State University, Institute of Management and Labor Relations
   and University Extension Division, December 1967.

3. The median income figure was not available for that
   same year.

4. Chernick, Indik, and Sternlieb, op. cit., p. 28.

5. Thomas R. Brooks, "Newark," The Atlantic, Vol. 224,
   No. 2, August 1969, pp. 4-12; p. 8.

6. Chernick, Indik, and Sternlieb, op. cit., p. 10.

7. Ibid., p. 3.

8. Ibid.

9. Ibid., p. 6.

10. Report for Action, Governor's Select Commission on
    Civil Disorder, State of New Jersey, February 1968,
    p. 20.

11. Ibid., p. 2.

12. Ibid., p. 3.

13. Even if we had wished to study the development of the
    child relative to his origins, the legal obstacles
    would have been formidable.

14. Puerto Ricans are underrepresented because of a short-
     age of Spanish speaking interviewers.

15. The N's are 407 and 404 respectively, and include men
     and women who married after the beginning of the
     study but exclude those study participants who did
     not marry before its end.

16. The ethnic breakdown by age of marriage included 188
     white women, 199 Negro women, 187 white men,
     and 197 Negro men.

17. N's for this analysis were 554 for women and 488 for
     men. Missing information, particularly on absent
     fathers, accounted for the differences between the
     figures and the sample total of 555.

18. This percentage would be larger if economically depen-
     dent families living with their own kin--no income
     estimates for families of procreation were available--
     were to be included.

19. According to the Rutgers study, 16.5% of the Newark
     families earned less than $3,000 and 58.4% less
     than $7,000 a year (as compared to 74.2% of the
     FLIP sample who earned less than $7,000).   See
     Chernick, Indik, and Sternlieb, op. cit. , p. 28.

20. Based on the William Wells adaptation of the Hollings-
     head Two Factor Index of Social Position.

21. N's are 524 and 408 respectively.   The requisite infor-
     mation on residence pattern was notably missing on
     out-of-wedlock and absent fathers.

Chapter 5

SOCIAL FUNCTIONING OF THE YOUNG URBAN FAMILIES

This chapter deals with the social functioning of the
555 families in the active study population at the start of the
research project. It should be recalled that at the first interview the families had only one child who was generally
less than a year old. Information about the family's social
functioning was based on interview data and observation in
the home during the initial visit. However, data pertaining
to the beginning situation were often revealed in subsequent
interviews or obtained from sources other than the family
itself, and these would be entered in the narrative covering
the beginning situation at a later time. Because of this, the
beginning situation was not evaluated until the family had been
part of the longitudinal research or treatment panel for at
least two years. This was an attempt to overcome the shortcomings inherent in a one-shot interview where the respondent might be slow at first contact to reveal information of a
sensitive nature. [1]

The reader can form a first overall picture of the
families' social functioning at the onset of the Project by
studying the distribution of total family functioning scores,
based on a summation of eight main categories of social
functioning. The ninth category, Relationship to the Social
Worker, is omitted here because it is not applicable at the
start of the Research Project; it becomes relevant later on
only to those cases which were randomly assigned to the
treatment group. The distribution shown in Table 3 represents behavior at an early stage of the family life cycle,
shortly after the birth of the first child and unaffected by
professional treatment programs except for a small handful
of cases (seven in all) who had availed themselves of the
services of a family or mental hygiene service. Beginning
social functioning scores also constitute a base line for the
study of change over time, to which we can compare modifications resulting both from the operation of normal social
forces impinging on the family and from the special services

set up by the Family Life Improvement Project to help the
families improve their functioning.

With scores in eight categories ranging from 1 or
inadequate to 7 or adequate functioning, the theoretical total
score range is from 8 to 56. However, the bulk of families
(98%) fell into a considerably narrower range of 33-56. This
restricted range of actual scores is related to the fact that
malfunctioning (scores below 4 or marginal functioning) rarely
occurs in all or nearly all categories of social functioning.
In the event that a family does seriously and continuously
malfunction in its major family roles, it ceases to be a
family. [2]

As seen in Table 3, the distribution of total functioning scores for our sample of normal young urban families
represents a highly skewed frequency curve, whose mode is
adequate or nearly adequate functioning. At the beginning
of the study 12% of the families were found to function adequately in all areas (scores of 56); nearly 10% were found
to function at a slightly above marginal level (scores of 32-
40); and less than 2% of the families could be characterized
as seriously malfunctioning; i.e., where behavior does not
violate laws but is potentially threatening to the welfare of
the individual or family (scores below 32). The remainder
of the families had scores ranging from above marginal to
adequate, with a decided skewing of cases at the adequate
end of the continuum. [3]

The median family functioning score was 50, indicating that half the families in the study sample were totally
adequate or manifested minor problematic functioning in one
to six areas or--less characteristically--more extensive
malfunctioning in one or two areas.

The distribution of scores for each of the main categories[4] of functioning is shown in Table 4. When each of the
eight areas was analyzed separately, the mean per cent of
families obtaining scores of 7 or adequate was 46.7 (as contrasted with only 12.1% obtaining overall ratings of adequate
in the total of all areas). The three areas showing the highest
level of adequacy were Use of Community Resources, Care
and Training of Children, and Family Relationships, with more
than half of the families in the study sample receiving ratings
of 7 or adequate. (These figures are 68.2, 56.9 and 50.1%,
respectively.)

Table 3

Frequency Distribution of Social Functioning
Scores for 555 Families at the Beginning
of the Study

Family Func- tioning Score*	Number of Families	Percent	Cumulative Percentages
56	67	12. 1	12. 1
55	47	8. 5	20. 6
54	52	9. 4	30. 0
53	45	8. 1	38. 1
52	38	6. 8	44. 9
51	29	5. 2	50. 1
50	34	6. 1	56. 2
49	36	6. 5	62. 7
48	28	5. 0	67. 7
47	21	3. 9	71. 6
46	25	4. 5	76. 1
45	22	4. 0	80. 1
44	20	3. 6	83. 7
43	13	2. 3	86. 0
42	9	1. 6	87. 6
41	13	2. 3	89. 9
40	7	1. 3	91. 2
39	8	1. 4	92. 6
38	8	1. 4	94. 0
37	7	1. 3	95. 3
36	9	1. 6	96. 9
35	3	. 5	97. 4
34	3	. 5	97. 9
33	2	. 4	98. 3
32	1	. 2	98. 5
13-31	8	1. 5	100. 0
	555	100. 0	

*Information was missing for three main categories.
In order to determine total score, the rating for
these categories was estimated as the mean value
of the other categories.

Table 4

Percentage Distribution of Study Families by Three Levels of Social Functioning

Area of Family Functioning	Percent of Families by Level of Functioning			
	Marginal & Below 1-4	Above Marginal & Near Adequate 5-6	Adequate 7	Total Number Cases*
Family Relationships & Unity	9. 6	40. 3	50. 1	555
Individual Behavior & Adjustment	8. 2	49. 0	42. 8	554
Care & Training of Children	4. 0	39. 1	56. 9	555
Social Activities	4. 0	53. 3	42. 7	555
Economic Practices	9. 6	47. 8	42. 6	554
Home & Household Practices	18. 4	46. 3	35. 3	555
Health Conditions & Practices	6. 2	58. 8	35. 0	555
Use of Community Resources	2. 2	29. 6	68. 2	554

*The total number of cases is 555 representing all study families who had beginning-of-study evaluation. N's less than 555 are due to missing data.

Marginal and below marginal functioning, that is, social functioning of a problematic nature representing behavior substantially at odds with community standards and an actual or potential threat to family welfare, was characteristic of 7.8% of the families when means or percentages are taken into account. The area ranking highest in the proportion of families obtaining scores of 4 and less (marginal and below-marginal) was Home and Household Practices, followed by Family Relationships and Unity, Economic Practices, and Individual Behavior and Adjustment. (The figures are 18.4, 9.6, 9.6 and 8.2%, respectively.)

The area by area analysis reveals somewhat more concentration of problemicity in areas which are instrumental rather than inter-personal, although that distribution is not clear-cut. The relatively extensive measure of instrumental problemicity would seem to be an indication of the families' low economic status in the community where the research was done. Unfortunately, no data are yet available which relate the patterns of functioning of representative samples of families to the communities' social structure. Limited comparison data suggest, nonetheless, that the present pattern may be more characteristic of Newark in the mid-sixties than of young urban families per se. [5]

Despite the relative class homogeneity of Newark families in general and our study sample in particular, a more microscopic inspection of the sample reveals sharp differences in social functioning when specific ethnic, marital status, and class differences are taken into account. For purposes of this analysis, the sample has been divided into four total score groupings, each comprising between 20% and 30% of the population. The groupings labeled by letter A, B, C, and D represent decreasing degrees of social functioning adequacy as shown below.

Total Score Groupings	No. of Cases	% of Cases
Grouping A (56-54) (Highest Social Functioning)	166	30.0
Grouping B (53-50)	146	26.2
Grouping C (49-46)	110	19.8
Grouping D (45-8) (Lowest Social Functioning)	133	24.0
Total	555	100.0

A comparison of Negro and Puerto Rican and white study families, omitting mixed marriages, reveals the following distribution:

Total Score Groupings	N=338 Negroes %	N=192 Whites %	N=23 Puerto Rican %
Grouping A	17.2	53.6	17.4
Grouping B	25.1	26.0	47.8
Grouping C	26.6	8.9	13.1
Grouping D	31.1	11.5	21.7

$$x^2 = 99.86, \ 6 \text{ d.f.}, \ p < .001$$

The modal distribution for Negro and white families are at opposite ends of the social functioning continuum, denoting very pronounced and statistically significant differences between Negro, Puerto Rican, and white families. These differences which appear consistently in all main categories and almost all sub-categories of family functioning are to no small extent, as we shall show below, a function of the pronounced social class differences between Negroes and Puerto Ricans, on the one hand, and whites, on the other. Differences between Negro and Puerto Rican families were below the 5% level of statistical significance ($x^2 = 6.32$, 3 d.f.).

The striking effect of social class upon the social functioning of the families is demonstrated in Table 5.

With social class seemingly the strong determinant of family functioning, as suggested by Table 5, how does class affect the relationship between Negroes and whites?[6] Table 6 gives a comparison of the social functioning of Negro and white families by total score groupings.

Table 6 leaves little doubt that the extremely strong association between race and class becomes attenuated as a result of the injection of class as a control factor. Differences between black and white families are statistically significant for the three status groups but of a lower magnitude in Class VI, composed largely of families headed by unskilled, unemployed, welfare parents.[7]

Table 5

Relationship Between Social Class and Family Functioning

Level of Social Functioning Percent of Families in Each Total Score Grouping	Index of Social Position		
	Class I-IV	Class V	Class VI
A	65.3	33.6	10.4
B	22.4	32.4	19.9
C	8.2	18.2	27.4
D	4.1	15.8	42.3
Total Percent	100.0	100.0	100.0
N	98	241	201

x^2 = 137.58, 6 d.f., p $<$ .001

Table 6

Negro and White Families Compared on Total Social Functioning Scores with Social Class Held Constant

(Ne = Negro; W = White)

Total Score Groupings	Class I-IV		Class V		Class VI	
	Ne	W	Ne	W	Ne	W
A	41.9	77.3	24.1	47.3	7.6	24.2
B	35.5	15.2	29.2	33.7	19.2	20.7
C	16.1	4.5	25.5	9.5	29.9	17.2
D	6.5	3.0	21.2	9.5	43.3	37.9
Total %	100.0	100.0	100.0	100.0	100.0	100.0
N's	31	66	137	95	157	29

Class I-IV x^2_2 = 12.05, 3 d.f., p $<$ .01
Class V x^2_2 = 21.73, 3 d.f., p $<$ .001
Class VI x^2 = 8.13, 3 d.f., p $<$ .05

This is partially in line with the cumulative evidence of three earlier studies relating black-white differences in social functioning to class. These point to sharp contrasts in Class V urban families, smaller and not necessarily statistically significant differences in urban highest status and lowest status families. Differences between black and white suburban families were found to be of a relatively low magnitude.

Families headed by out-of-wedlock mothers functioned much less well than two-parent families. In view of the fact that almost all families with out-of-wedlock children were Negro, a comparison of Negro families headed by married mothers with Negro families headed by unmarried mothers provides a more accurate measure of the correlates of out-of-wedlock status. [8] (The opportunity to compare the functioning of white O. W.'s is seriously limited by the fact that there were only five cases of the latter in the sample. [9]) Data on the foregoing groups are shown below:

Family Functioning Total Score Groupings	Negro Married	Negro O. W.	White O. W.
A	30. 0	4. 4	
B	27. 6	21. 7	
C	23. 6	30. 4	20. 0
D	18. 8	43. 5	80. 0
Total	100. 0	100. 0	100. 0
N	170	161	5

X^2 for Negro Married and O. W. = 49. 99, 3 d. f. , p $<$. 001

Negro families headed by married parents function significantly more adequately than Negro families headed by unmarried mothers reflecting very pronounced social and economic differences[10] between the two groups. The five white families headed by unmarried mothers register much more problematic social functioning than the Negro unmarried mothers. We cannot, of course, assess how representative these five cases may be. Our rough data indicate, however, that the white unmarried mothers were economically less well off than their black counterparts. [11] Moreover, white unmarried mothers who kept their child may have found themselves more stigmatized and this may be reflected in family functioning.

As a last aspect of this analysis of family functioning correlates, the relationship between the social functioning of the young families or procreation and their respective families of origin was investigated. Kirkpatrick has compiled some evidence relating the marital adjustment of the young couple to the happiness of their parents' marriages.[12] In an earlier study the senior author showed a high measure of continuity in social status as well as family functioning from one generation to the next.[13] The search for correlates of family functioning in the structure and behavior of the families of origin, if rewarded by significant findings, holds promise for extending the presently narrow frontiers of prevention, because parental behavior is observable and measurable and accessible to intervention before the children have been launched.

Information on families of orientation was not nearly so rich as on our families of procreation. For many reasons data on the paternal families were often missing--the mother may not know her in-laws or the father may not have told his wife much about his own family background. The question of data validity can rightfully be posed here since memory, which rarely functions without a flaw, figures prominently in the gathering of retrospective data. Still and all, while conceding the greater likelihood of data distortion, the validity of information on families of procreation demonstrated in this and previous projects does not lead us to believe that data on families of origin are invalid.

Employing three levels of functioning for families of orientation (represented by Roman numerals I, II, and III, in order of most to least adequate functioning) we examined the relationship between beginning level of functioning of the study family and that of the families of origin.[14] This is shown in Table 7.

The distribution of percentages leaves no doubt that there is a substantial association between the functioning of the two generations of families. The gamma correlation is +.58 for maternal family and +.42 for paternal family, both relationships being statistically significant much beyond the .001 level. Whether the lower coefficient for fathers' families represents a substantive difference in association between the variables or is the result of incompleteness of data is not known at this stage. The findings presented here, replicating as they do this type of analysis with other samples, strongly support the contention that there is a high

Table 7

Relationship Between the Social Functioning of Families of Orientation and Procreation

Family of Procreation	Maternal Family Percentages				Paternal Family Percentages			
	Most Ade. I	II	Least Ade. III	Total N	Most Ade. I	II	Least Ade. III	Total N
Most Adequate A	54.7	31.0	10.5	164	57.0	37.6	23.4	147
B	26.7	32.8	19.6	141	25.2	32.5	22.5	97
C	13.0	20.1	23.9	106	10.4	12.8	24.3	56
D Least Adequate	5.6	16.1	46.0	133	7.4	17.1	29.8	63
%	100.0	100.0	100.0		100.0	100.0	100.0	
Total N	161	174	209	544	135	117	111	363

$X^2 = 138.63$, 6 d.f. p $< .001$

$X^2 = 45.60$, 6 d.f. p $< .001$

measure of continuity in social functioning between family of origin and family of procreation. It should be remembered, nevertheless, that hardly a third of the variance in the functioning of young families can be explained by the functioning of their own parental families. There are a variety of other variables shaping the nature of family functioning. At the same time, it must be said that the identification of one factor shaping the nature of family life is an important step forward in the unravelling of the problem of causation in family malfunctioning.

1. This issue first aroused the attention of the writers in the New Haven Neighborhood Improvement Project where score discrepancies between first and subsequent panel interviews led to an analysis of the narrative content of the research protocols. It was found that frequently data pertaining to the beginning situation were entered by the interviewers in later protocols and therefore omitted from the evaluation of the beginning situation. The study, but not this particular methodological problem, is reported in Geismar and Krisberg, The Forgotten Neighborhood, pp. 318-353.

2. Even the seriously disorganized or multi-problem families, which have been the subject of many studies, generally reveal some areas of strength or adequacy defined as functioning at or above the marginal level. See Geismar, "Family Functioning as an Index of Need for Welfare Services," loc. cit., pp. 99-113.

3. It should be remembered that the family functioning scale used here was designed for a population of malfunctioning families who distribute themselves in a manner more nearly approaching a normal curve. (See Geismar and Ayres, op. cit., p. 26.) Furthermore, it is likely that the young age of families also contributed to the skewing of the distribution. (See Geismar, Preventive Intervention in Social Work, pp. 58-70.) The lower percentage of adequately functioning families in the present study as compared to the foregoing piece of research should be mentioned. The difference is the result of some revisions in the definitions of adequate functioning leading to a less frequent assignment of the score of "7". The revised rating scheme is contained in Geismar, Family and Community Functioning.

4. The researchers examined the interrelationship of total
    and category scores. The Guttman scale, which is
    the preferred technique for determining this, was not
    applicable here as it was in studies with more prob-
    lematic populations because of the spacing and distri-
    bution of category scores. (See Geismar, LaSorte,
    and Ayres, loc. cit.) An alternate procedure was fol-
    lowed. Pearsonian coefficients of the intercorrelation
    of main category and total scores were calculated.
    The matrix is shown in Appendix D.   The coefficients
    leave no doubt that the scale items hang together and
    are significantly related to the total score.   Even in
    the absence of unidimensionality, the types of roles
    and forms of social functioning that we have been
    measuring show a degree of association which makes
    it possible to relate them meaningfully to the overall
    dependent variable of this study, the social functioning
    of the family. It may be of interest to those concerned
    with the methodology of measurement to learn that
    concurrent with the writing of the present manuscript
    the sub-categories of the family functioning scale for
    FLIP data were subjected to factor analysis.   Ortho-
    gonal rotation of the principal component method yield-
    ed three major factors, the interpersonal-expressive,
    the instrumental, and the economic.   This categori-
    zation corresponds rather closely to the conceptuali-
    zation used in the analysis of the service input in
    Chapter 7 (for further details turn to Chapter 7).

5. See Geismar, Preventive Intervention in Social Work,
    pp. 29-36; 58-70.

6. Puerto Ricans, underrepresented because of a shortage
    of Spanish speaking interviewers, are omitted from
    the multiple variable analyses.   It was found that
    Negroes and Puerto Ricans do not differ significantly
    in family functioning.

7. L. L. Geismar and Ursula Gerhart, "On Social Class,
    Ethnicity, and Family Functioning," Journal of Mar-
    riage and the Family, Vol. 30, No. 3, August 1968,
    pp. 480-487. See also in Letters to the Editor De-
    partment of same periodical, Vol. 31, No. 3, August
    1969, William J. Parish, Jr. , "On Social Class,
    Ethnicity, and Family Functioning," pp. 429-430;
    and L. L. Geismar and Ursula Gerhart, "Reply to
    William J. Parish, Jr. ," pp. 430-431.

8. The word correlate rather than effect is used here, be-
    cause we are in no position to assess the reciprocal
    cause and effect relationship between illegitimacy and
    social functioning.

9. In addition to differences between Negroes and whites in
    social class distribution, differential opportunities for
    the placement of children are seen as the major
    causes of the differences in the O. W. rates.

10. Of married Negro families 16% were in Class I-IV, 60%
    in Class V, and 24% in Class VI. The comparable fig-
    ures for the families of black unwed mothers were 3%,
    23%, and 74%. The mean scores for source of income,
    which is a compound measure of both the amount and
    source of income (i. e. , from work vs. public assis-
    tance) is 6. 19 for the Negro married and 5. 19 for the
    Negro O. W. 's.

11. The mean scores for source of income were 5. 19 for
    black O. W. families and 4. 80 for white ones.

12. Clifford Kirpatrick, "Measuring Marital Adjustment,"
    Robert F. Winch, et al. (eds.), Selected Studies in
    Marriage and the Family, New York: Holt, Rinehart
    and Winston, 1962, pp. 544-553.

13. Geismar, Preventive Intervention in Social Work, pp.
    43-46.

14. The procedure used to rate the social functioning of the
    families of orientation was a modification of that
    used for the young families themselves, because data
    on the former were rather poor.   Coders followed
    the same procedure in rating families of origin as
    they did in rating families of procreation with one
    difference.   Instead of rating each area of family
    functioning separately, they rated total family func-
    tioning in terms of the expressive and instrumental
    dimensions and assigned separate scores to each.
    This procedure was resorted to in order to make
    coding possible even where information on score cat-
    egories of social functioning was missing.   No coding
    was done where data on those two dimensions were
    scarce.   Of 555 families in the experimental and
    control groups at the start of the study, 544 could
    be rated on maternal family but only 363 on paternal

family of origin.   The lower figure for rating the
parents of fathers can be explained in part by the
absence of fathers in out-of-wedlock cases.

Ratings for the parental families were done separately on a five-point scale (the scale points were
adequate, marginal plus, marginal, marginal minus,
and inadequate) for instrumental and expressive roles,
and the two were combined later to constitute a
three-point continuum as follows: category I comprising adequate ratings in both instrumental and
expressive roles;   category II covering adequate or
marginal plus in one role, marginal plus in the
other, or adequate in one and marginal and lower
in the other;   category III covering marginal plus
or marginal and less in one type of role and marginal or less in the other.

Chapter 6

CHANGES IN FAMILY FUNCTIONING
RELATED TO THE PROGRAM OF SERVICES

A major portion of the Family Life Improvement Project was devoted to studying the effects of a program of professional intervention upon a sub-sample of the young families in the original research. Eight college educated individuals under the close supervision of trained and experienced professional social workers carried out the program of intervention, which will be discussed in detail in Chapter 7.

As described in an earlier chapter, random sampling techniques were employed to select the control and experimental groups. This technique was chosen because it established two groups essentially alike in family functioning and social characteristics, with only one receiving Project services. Thus, subsequent differences in functioning between the two groups noted after a three year period could be attributed to the effect of treatment given or withheld.

A comparison of the 175 control and 177 treatment families at the beginning of the Project on the independent variable family functioning and on selected social characteristics reveals that despite attrition they were, in fact, basically similar.[1] (See in Appendix A a comparison of treatment and control groups on beginning score and selected demographic variables.)

With equivalence established in the starting position, changes in functioning between experimental and control groups during the period of treatment can be meaningfully compared. Changes in overall functioning and in the eight separate categories will be examined in relation to each other; changes in the sample as a whole and for various sub-samples will also be scrutinized. Finally, a comparative analysis of the patterns of change exhibited by the experimental and control groups will be carried out.

Before we present the findings, a word or two about the statistical analysis is in order. Two statistical measures were relied upon to assess the strength and significance of the relationship between given variables. Gamma[2] was calculated in order to gauge the strength of the relationship and chi square[3] was obtained to assess statistical significance. The closer the gamma is to unity, the stronger the relationship. A gamma falling below $\pm.3$ was considered indicative of a weak relationship. The relationship was judged to be statistically significant when the chi square probability reached .05 or less. For certain findings discussed below, tables in their entirety are presented. With respect to other findings, only gamma and levels of chi square probabilities are shown (for the sake of simplification).

Overall Movement

In order to obtain a macroscopic view of the effects of the program of intervention, the degree of total movement occurring during the treatment period was compared for both experimental and control families. Measurement for both groups covers the time from the first research interview to the last contact at the end of the study. Movement was differentiated into five categories, two of positive, two of negative, and one of zero movement. The comparison is presented in Table 8.

Table 8. Percent of Families in
Treatment and Control Group by Overall Movement

Movement	Treatment (N=177)	Control (N=175)
High positive (4 or more points)	27.7	18.3
Low positive (1 to 3 points)	20.9	21.1
No movement	13.0	13.7
Low negative (1 to 3 points)	18.1	25.1
High negative (4 or more points)	20.3	21.7
Total	100.0	100.0

x^2 = 5.53, 4 d.f., p < .30
gamma = +.137

*Due to a rounding off procedure of computer supplied data, percentages may not add up exactly to 100%.

Table 8 reveals small, non-significant differences, reflecting somewhat greater improvement for the treatment families when compared to the control group. [4] The modal movement pattern of served families is in a positive direction while that of families not served is in a negative direction. A closer look at degree of change shows that treatment families are more likely than control families to register high positive movement (27. 7% compared to 18. 3%) and at the same time less likely to exhibit low negative movement (18. 1% compared with 25. 1%). The relative proportion of experimental and control families within each of the remaining categories of movement is nearly identical.

Movement in Eight Areas of Family Functioning

Given the foregoing findings of positive movement on the part of treatment families, we must ask whether total score differences reflect an internal pattern of separate area differences in the same direction or an aggregate of up and down differences which happen to balance out in a particular direction. If the former is in evidence, a case can be made for the presence of forces that have been operating to bring about changes in this particular direction. Table 9 presents a comparison of changes in family functioning between experimental and control groups according to the eight main categories of social functioning. As noted in Table 9 the predominant outcome is zero change in both control and experimental groups. When other than zero changes are considered, seven out of eight categories in the experimental group as against three out of eight categories in the control group show a net balance of unweighted positive over negative change.

In all areas but one, Use of Community Resources, the treatment group families fared at least minimally better than control group families. In the Use of Community Resources area the reverse is true, with control group families performing slightly better at the end of the treatment period than experimental group families.

In three of the eight areas of family functioning, in the categories Care and Training of Children, Home and Household Practices, and Health Conditions and Practices, the treated families did significantly better than the untreated families. [5] A more detailed inspection of the shifts that occurred in each of the three areas above enables us to identify more precisely the nature of the changes that took place.

Table 9. Experimental and Control Groups Compared on Movement by Main Category of Family Functioning*(Given in Percentages)

Family Functioning Areas	Experimental Group(N=177)					Control Group(N=175)					Gamma	P-level Chi Square
	High pos. (2 pts. +)	Low pos. (1 pt.)	No Ch.	Low neg. (1 pt.)	High neg. (2 pts. +)	High pos. (2 pts. +)	Low pos. (1 pt.)	No Ch.	Low neg. (1 pt.)	High neg. (2 pts. +)		
Family Relat. & Unity	9.0	19.2	46.3	12.4	13.0	8.0	16.6	49.1	14.9	11.4	+.040	$p < .90$
Indiv. Behav. & Adjustment	6.8	23.7	43.5	16.4	9.6	5.1	20.6	48.0	15.4	10.9	+.060	$p < .90$
Care/Training of Children	4.0	16.9	45.2	21.5	12.4	0.6	13.1	37.7	27.4	21.1	+.248	$p < .05$
Social Activities	5.6	29.9	44.6	12.4	7.3	4.6	18.9	56.0	13.1	7.4	+.148	$p < .20$
Economic Practices	10.2	16.4	49.7	15.8	7.9	8.6	15.4	44.6	24.0	7.4	+.101	$p < .50$
Home & Household Practices	20.9	14.7	41.2	15.3	7.9	9.1	20.6	43.4	14.9	12.0	+.142	$p < .05$
Health Conditions/Practices	5.1	18.1	55.9	11.9	9.0	4.6	21.1	40.0	28.0	6.3	+.097	$p < .01$
Community Resources Use	4.0	13.6	70.6	7.9	4.0	4.0	16.6	69.1	8.6	1.7	-.085	$p < .80$

* The range of change scores for main areas of functioning was much narrower than that of overall functioning, necessitating the use of a different set of cutting points for the two levels of positive and negative movement than those used for total movement (Table 8).

In the category Care and Training of Children, there was an overall trend toward more problematic functioning in both the experimental and control groups. Negative movement, however, was considerably more pronounced among the control group and is reflected in the fact that these families showed a higher proportion of deterioration labelled high negative (2 or more points) as well as low negative (1 point).

Focusing on the two components of Care and Training of Children, a) Training Methods and Emotional Care, and b) Physical Care, we find that treatment group gains were greater in both sub-categories and particularly pronounced in Training Methods and Emotional Care (see Table 10).

Table 10. Comparison of Treatment and
Control Families with Respect to Movement in Two
Sub-categories of Care and Training of Children

Movement*	Training Methods and Emotional Care		Physical Care	
	Treatment Families %	Control Families %	Treatment Families %	Control Families %
Positive	20.2	11.6	19.3	15.5
No Change	44.5	33.5	67.1	67.3
Negative	35.3	54.9	13.6	17.2
	100.0	100.0	100.0	100.0
Total N	176	174	176	174

Gamma = +.336   Gamma = +.125
Chi Square = 14.18, 2 d.f.   Chi Square = 1.46, 2 d.f.,
p < .001   p < .50

*To facilitate the analysis, the five degrees of movement were collapsed into three.

This apparently constitutes an area of family functioning where problems occur as part of the developmental process by which the child is transformed from a post-uterine, passive, and, by and large, non-problematic object into a psycho-social being, energetically interacting with his environment and prone to problematic behavior. During the early stages of child development, intervention in the area

of Care and Training of Children means coping, through preventive or remedial action, with problems which are very
much part of the child's growth and development process.
It would appear that this is the one area in which the FLIP
worker was most effective, possibly because a prevention-
geared service has a greater effectiveness when malfunctioning is a likely occurrence, as it was in child care.

The more favorable outcome of the treatment over the
control group in the area of Home and Household Practices
is represented by a different movement pattern.   In this category we are struck by the higher proportion of treatment
families showing marked improvement (2 or more points)
while differences between the two groups are relatively small
in other levels of movement.   An inspection of sub-categories
shows that this difference is due largely to improved housing
(the Project invested a great deal of effort in helping clients
improve their housing situation) rather than better household
practices (see Table 11).

In Health Conditions and Practices, the third category
showing significant movement for treatment cases, intervention appears to have had the effect of preventing more problematic functioning rather than bringing about improvement.
Families in the control group are more prone than those in
the treatment group to move toward greater malfunctioning,
but this movement is likely to be of a relatively small magnitude (1 point).   The more frequent occurrence of health problems as well as poorer health practices related to the use of
medical and dental practitioners and facilities accounted for
the poorer performance of the control group (see Table 12).

It is interesting that, like Care and Training of Children, Health Conditions and Practices is both an area of likely
malfunctioning (it ranks second in negative change for control
families) and relatively effective intervention.   This suggests
the possibility of a relationship existing between the two sets
of factors.

A Look at the Movement of Different Groups of Families Comprising the Sample

In the last ten years a sizable quantity of evidence[6]
has accumulated pointing toward the fact that insight-oriented
psychotherapy (which to the present has constituted the basic
framework of casework) has failed to help the large segment
of the population which is in the lower echelons of socio-
economic status.   The theme that runs through most of this

Table 11. Comparison of Treatment and
Control Families with Respect to Movement in Two Sub-
Categories of Home and Household Practices

	Physical Facilities		Housekeeping Standards	
Movement	Treatment Families %	Control Families %	Treatment Families %	Control Families %
Positive	41.5	31.0	29.5	24.7
No Change	38.6	44.3	56.8	57.5
Negative	19.9	24.7	13.6	17.8
Total N	176	174	176	174

Gamma = +.172
Chi Square = 4.21, 2 d.f.,
p < .20

Gamma = +.124
Chi Square = 1.73, 2 d.f.,
p < .50

Table 12. Comparison of Treatment and
Control Families with Respect to Movement in Two Sub-
Categories of Health Conditions and Practices

	Health Conditions		Health Practices	
Movement	Treatment Families %	Control Families %	Treatment Families %	Control Families %
Positive	21.0	17.2	27.1	31.8
No Change	52.3	46.0	55.4	43.9
Negative	26.7	36.8	17.5	24.3
Total N	176	174	176	174

Gamma = +.172
Chi Square = 4.16, 2 d.f.,
p < .20

Gamma = +.017
Chi Square = 4.87, 2 d.f.,
p < .10

work is that the failure is largely the result of certain attitudinal, cognitive, and behavioral traits which are characteristic of the lower-class population.

Briefly, the gist of the various findings is as follows:

a) Lower-class individuals, compared to those of the
middle and upper classes, are less likely to avail themselves
of this kind of help.

b) When lower-class clients reach an agency offering this
kind of help, there is a good chance that they will either be
rejected by the agency, prematurely drop out of treatment, or
participate in the therapy in an inappropriate manner.

c) A variety of reasons are offered to account for (a)
and (b). These can be classified under two major headings:
(1) reasons that relate to the client's perspective toward
psycho-social problems, and (2) those that pertain to his
lack of knowledge about the treatment process. With regard
to the first, lower-class clients are likely to view emotional
problems in somatic terms; they want concrete assistance
and immediate changes; they are not likely to search for
underlying causes and/or favor the use of deterrent measures
to cope with undesirable behavior. As to the latter set of
reasons, most frequently cited is the client's expectation that
the therapist will act authoritatively while he responds in a
passive manner.

Mayer and Timms offer a description of what the
working-class client expects will take place during treatment.[7]
According to them the client typically expected to present an
account of his problems in one or two sessions after which
the worker would reach a conclusion based upon principles of
right and wrong. The client would be advised how to change
the offender's behavior, instructed to act in a particular way
or to use deterrent measures.

The studies cited agree that orientation discrepancies
between worker and client result in considerable frustration
for both and render the probability of a successful treatment
outcome highly unlikely.

Many of the studies attribute the client's perspective
to basic orientations that are grounded in the socio-cultural
milieu of the lower socio-economic groups. Most frequently

mentioned are a limited capacity to verbalize and/or think in symbolic terms, an orientation toward the present rather than the future, a moralistic-unicausal perspective toward behavior, and a sense of powerlessness with respect to the underlying conditions of existence.

The social work literature has devoted considerable attention to those clients situated at the lowest end of the social ladder, sometimes referred to as the "multi-problem" family. They are characterized by extensive problemicity in a great many aspects of life and by the persistence of these problems over long periods of time, perhaps for the life time of family members and sometimes even extending over several generations. Although their need for services is most urgent, these families tend to reject or resist help. They not only share with other individuals of lower socio-economic status those traits described previously which tend to serve as barriers to effective treatment, they are also likely to exhibit an antipathy toward most of society's institutions, thus placing an additional obstacle in the way of effective services. [8]

Oscar Lewis deals with some of the characteristics ascribed to the "multi-problem" family, but his analysis casts individuals and families into a broader theoretical framework which he terms the culture of poverty, [9] describing it as a "subculture of Western society with its own structure and rationale, a way of life handed on from generation to generation along family lines."[10] He identifies the structural and economic conditions under which a culture of poverty is likely to develop, and describes the families belonging to this subculture with their tendency to exhibit a remarkable similarity in life styles, values, orientations, and relationships with both the subculture and the large society, regardless of the ethnic group to which they may belong or country in which they may reside. According to Lewis, the poor Negro in American cities, the poor white in Appalachia, the poverty stricken Puerto Rican in San Juan and New York, and the Mexican slum dweller all exhibit a great many similarities not because of parallels in the history of their people but because of their common membership in the culture of poverty which is both a response and adaptation to occupying a marginal position in society. Lewis delineates four major characteristics of this culture, some of which have been noted previously as characterizing the "multi-problem" family: (1) a disengagement from and hostility to the major institutions of society; (2) a low level of organization among the poor themselves; (3) a high proportion of families in which the father is absent; and (4) a distinctive set of personality traits which stem from having grown up in the culture. These include a sense of fatalism, powerlessness, inferiority, an orientation toward the present, and a marked capacity to endure psychological pathology.

It is the contention of the preceding literature that the traditional approaches of casework are relatively ineffective in helping individuals and families who belong to lower socioeconomic status groups and it is suggested that the explanation for this lies in the socio-cultural milieu in which the individual lives which provides him with a set of attitudinal, cognitive, and behavioral characteristics making it highly unlikely that he will benefit from this type of help. Either implicit or explicit in much of this literature is the position that strategies for coping with the problems of individuals of lower socio-economic status must be brought more closely into line with their special, class-related orientations.

The Family Life Improvement Project departed in many ways from traditional casework procedure. Although we reserve the details for the next chapter, it should be noted that FLIP was unique in a number of ways: It reached out to families in their home; subjects felt that they were not only clients but participants in a research project; the objective of the service program was to provide help to clients over a total range of individual and family problems; workers accorded as much weight to problems of a concrete nature as they did to those of an intra- and interpersonal nature; and workers under close supervision were encouraged to select from a wide range of approaches those most suited to the needs expressed by the client. This approach to treatment, it was felt, would at least partially overcome some of the barriers to effective casework with lower-class clients which were noted earlier. We anticipated that it would facilitate the lower-class client's participation in the helping process, contribute to the establishment of a good relationship with the worker, bring the worker and client perspectives closer together in delineating problems and finding methods of coping, and that the end product would be an improvement in family functioning.

The deliberate efforts of the FLIP program to overcome certain limitations of traditional social work programs in relation to helping clients from the more marginal groups in society, together with the finding of a modicum of overall

and category movement of treatment families for the sample
as a whole prompted the researchers to examine the effect
of intervention upon the various sub-groups comprising the
sample.

In order to do this, a comparison was made of the
movement of treatment and control group families, holding
constant beginning scores, social class, ethnic group membership, marital status, and the level of functioning of the
family in which the mother of the study family grew up. To
simplify the analysis and maximize the number of cases included in each subgroup, we collapsed the five categories of
movement into three: positive movement, no change, and
negative movement. Data are shown where the gamma
equals ±.3 or more and/or a chi square probability of .05
or less is obtained.

A.   LEVEL OF BEGINNING FUNCTIONING
     and the Effectiveness of Services

Three levels of beginning functioning were established,
representing functioning which was most adequate, moderately adequate, and least adequate. (The scale positions
included within each of the three levels of family functioning
for total score and area or main category score is shown
at the end of the chapter in note 11.)

For each level of initial functioning, treatment and
control families were compared with regard to overall movement and change within each area of family functioning.[12]

The data suggest that the program of services was
somewhat more effective for those families functioning at the
outset of the study at either the high and low ends of the
social functioning continuum than it was for those occupying
a middle position. This is substantiated by the data pertaining to the shifts occurring in the categories of functioning
rather than to the changes in the total score.

Families functioning at the least adequate level at the
beginning of the study. The differences which were found in
changes in the total score between treatment and control
group families which were most problematic at the beginning
of the study were approximately equivalent to the observed
differences between treatment and control group in the less

problematic families.   The outcome for the treatment group
was slightly more favorable than for the control group.   This
is reflected in a gamma of +.179.

The treatment group fared at least minimally better
than the control group in six of eight categories and considerably better in three of these areas.   The three areas in which
treated families registered considerably more positive movement than control families were Care and Training of Children,
Economic Practices, and Home and Household Practices. None
of these relationships, however, reached a level of statistical
significance, the probability level of the chi squares falling above
the .05 level.   Nevertheless, gammas ranged from moderate to
high as follows:

Category	Gamma	Chi Square Probability Level	Total Number Cases
Care/Training of Children	+.667	p< .10, 2 d.f.	18
Economic Practices	+.492	p< .30, 2 d.f.	35
Home and House- hold Practices	+.364	p< .30, 2 d.f.	72

Families functioning at a moderately adequate level
at the start.   Among those families functioning at a moderately adequate level at the onset of the project, treatment
families fared slightly but not significantly better than control families with respect to total score.   The gamma obtained was +.127.

A breakdown by categories of functioning shows the
treatment group with a more positive outcome than the control group in four of the areas and more negative outcome
in the remaining four.   In a single category, Social Activities, the outcome was significantly better for the treatment
group when compared with the control group.   On the other
hand, the treatment families did considerably worse than the
control families in Use of Community Resources.   On the
latter category, the gamma obtained was moderately high
but the chi square probability just misses the .05 level of
significance.   Gammas and chi square probability levels

obtained for the categories Social Activities and Use of Community Resources are shown below.

Category	Gamma	Chi Square Probability Level	Total Number Cases
Social Activities	+.261	p < .05, 2 d. f.	196
Use of Community Resources	-.419	p < .10, 2 d. f.	94

Families functioning most adequately at the beginning of the study. When changes in total scores were examined the differences between treatment and control groups were slight and statistically non-significant although the treatment group was placed in a more favorable position with regard to overall movement. A gamma of +.136 was obtained.

For specific categories of functioning, in five out of eight areas the treatment group did at least minimally better than the control group. In the three areas of Care and Training of Children, Economic Practices, and Health Conditions and Practices the differences were significant. Put another way, those families to whom services were provided were better able to maintain a relatively high level of functioning in the latter three areas than the control group. Gammas and chi square probability levels relative to each of the latter three areas are shown below:

Category	Gamma	Chi Square Probability Level	Total Number Cases
Care/Training of Children	+.337	p<.02, 1 d. f.	196
Economic Practices	+.516	p<.01, 1 d. f.	142
Health Conditions/Practices	+.704	p<.001, 1 d. f.	126

Summary. The program of intervention appeared to be somewhat more effective for families which, at the outset, functioned at the lowest and highest levels than for those whose initial functioning fell in the middle range. This is best depicted in Summary Chart A.

In addition to the three areas of Child Care and Training, Home and Household Practices, and Health Conditions and Practices which proved to be areas of effectiveness for the sample as a whole when beginning level of functioning was held constant, Economic Practices and Social Activities also emerged as areas of change for certain groups of families. Furthermore, with respect to the category Use of Community Resources, the program appeared to have an adverse effect on those treatment families whose beginning functioning was at a moderately adequate level, for they showed relatively greater deterioration at the end of the study than similar control families.

B. SOCIAL STATUS and the Effect of Intervention

Treatment and control groups were compared for overall and area movement at each of three levels of social status, the highest represented by Classes I to IV, the next highest by Class V, and the lowest by Class VI. Classes I to IV were combined in order to have a large enough sub-sample of families at the higher levels of social status [based on William Wells' adaptation of the Hollingshead Two Factor Index of Social Position].

The results of the analysis suggest that families of Classes V and VI were helped by the FLIP project to a slightly greater extent than families of Class I to IV.

Class I - IV families. Among higher status families the percentage of those treated whose total scores registered positive movement exceeded the percentage of families with positive movement in the control group. The difference, however, was not statistically significant, and the gamma obtained was of a relatively small magnitude (+.179).

As for categories of functioning, the project's end found treatment families of this social status performing at least slightly better than control families in four out of eight areas. In not a single area did the difference between the groups reach a magnitude that was statistically significant. Gammas fell below ±.20 except for the category Social Activities, for which a gamma of +.285 was obtained.

Summary Chart A

	Families with lowest beginning scores	Families with middle range beginning scores	Families with highest beginning scores
a. Treatment group made more gains than control group on total score	Yes	Yes	Yes
b. Was the difference in total score considerable (p of chi square $\leq .05$ and/or gamma $\geq +.3$)?	No	No	No
c. Number of areas in which treatment group did better than control group	6	4	5
d. Number of areas in which treatment group did considerably better (p of chi square $\leq .05$ and/or gamma $\geq +.3$)	3	1	3
e. Number of areas in which treatment group did more poorly than control group*	2	4	3
f. Number of areas in which treatment group did considerably more poorly (chi square p level $\leq .05$ and/or gamma $\geq -.3$)	0	1	0

* To avoid overburdening the reader with details the data on the number of areas in which the treatment group performed minimally more poorly than the control group are omitted from the narrative.

Class V families.   Like those at the higher level,
treatment families of this social class did somewhat but not
significantly better than control families with respect to total
score movement (gamma = +.186).   When, however, we
analyze categories of functioning, we find that treatment families in Class V did at least minimally better than control
families in five out of eight areas and considerably better in
two.   The two areas of greatest effectiveness were Care and
Training of Children and Health Conditions and Practices.
Gammas and chi square probabilities obtained for the latter
categories are shown below:

Category	Gamma	Chi Square Probability Level	Total Number Cases
Care/Training of Children	+.316	p < .10, 2 d.f.	148
Health Conditions/Practices	+.204	p < .01, 2 d.f.	148

Class VI families.   The total movement scores of
treatment and control families in Class VI reflect a pattern
similar to that of families at the higher social status levels.
The treatment group did better than the control group, but
the differences that were found were small and not statistically significant.   (A gamma of +.102 was obtained.)

On the other hand, the area by area analysis shows
that in seven of the eight areas treatment families of this
social class did at least minimally better than control families, and in one area, Care and Training of Children, the
difference between treatment and control groups was of a
considerable magnitude and nearly reached a level of statistical significance.   (Gamma = +.317; chi square probability
level < .10; 2 d.f., N = 147.)

Summary.   The evidence points toward the conclusion
that the program of services was of greater benefit to families in Classes V and VI than to those in Classes I-IV. This
is evidenced in Summary Chart B.

In contrast to the examination of the sample as a
whole, the comparison of treatment and control families at
each level of social status disclosed fewer areas in which

the outcome was significantly better for the treatment than for the control group.

Summary Chart B

	Class I-IV families	Class V families	Class VI families
a. Treatment group made more gains than control group on total score	Yes	Yes	Yes
b. Was the difference in total score considerable (chi square p level $\leq .05$ and/or gamma $\geq \pm .3$)?	No	No	No
c. Number of areas in which treatment group did better than control group	4	5	7
d. Number of areas in which treatment group did considerably better (chi square $p \leq .05$ and/ or gamma $\geq +.3$)	0	2	1
e. Number of areas in which treatment group did more poorly than control group	4	3	1
f. Numbers of areas in which treatment group did considerably more poorly (chi square p level $\leq .05$ and/or gamma $\geq -.3$)	0	0	0

C.   INITIAL PROBLEMICITY AND CLASS
     Related to Treatment Outcome

Carrying the evaluation of the program of intervention one step further, a comparison of the relative movement of treatment and control group families was made for combined

beginning score and social class.   In Chapter 5, it was noted
that a negative relationship existed between initial problemicity and class.   To separate the effects of the two variables,
we compared the two groups of families holding constant various combinations of social status and beginning score.

The findings that emerged from this analysis suggest
that the program of services was of greatest benefit to Class
VI families whose social functioning was adequate at the start
of the project and of next most benefit to Class V families,
also at the maximum level of functioning at the outset.

Class V families with adequate beginning scores.   A
comparison of changes in total scores for Class V families
which functioned adequately at the start of the study indicates
that greater overall gains were made by treated families compared with untreated families, but that the differences were
relatively small and statistically nonsignificant.   (A gamma
of +. 20 was obtained.)

When comparisons are made on separate categories
of functioning, the outcome was more favorable for treatment
cases than for control cases in five out of eight categories.
In three of these five categories the treatment group registered significantly more positive change than the control group.
These three areas are Care and Training of Children, Economic Practices, and Health Conditions and Practices.   Gammas and levels of chi square probability for each of the three
areas are presented below:

Category	Gamma	Chi Square Probability Level	Total Number Cases
Care/Training of Children	+. 442	p <. 05, 1 d.f.	89
Economic Practices	+. 564	p <. 02, 1 d.f.	76
Health Conditions/Practices	+. 747	p <. 01, 1 d.f.	60

Class VI families with adequate beginning scores.
Treatment and control families of this social status/beginning
score level exhibited only minor differences in total score

movement.   The very minimal edge of the treatment group
over the control group is evident in the +. 083 gamma.

A totally different picture emerges from an analysis
of movement within the eight categories of functioning. Treatment families fared better than control families in seven out
of eight areas.

In four areas, Care and Training of Children, Home
and Household Practices, Health Conditions and Practices,
and Economic Practices, the differences between treatment
and control are reflected in fairly high gammas and are statistically significant with the exception of the last category.
In two additional categories, Family Relationships and Individual Behavior and Adjustment, considerable differences
were observed between treatment and control groups although
somewhat less marked than in the foregoing instance and below the level of statistical significance.   Gammas and chi
square probability levels with respect to the categories discussed are shown below:

Category	Gamma	Chi Square Probability Level	Total Number Cases
Health Conditions & Practices	+.925	$p < .001$, 1 d. f.	35
Home and House-hold Practices	+.750	$p = .03*$, 1 d. f.	26
Economic Practices	+.742	$p = .06*$, 1 d. f.	21
Care/Training of Children	+.501	$p < .05$, 1 d. f.	61
Individual Behavior & Adjustment	+.362	$p < .30$, 1 d. f.	34
Family Relation-ships & Unity	+.322	$p < .30$, 1 d. f.	46

*Fisher's Exact Probability Test.

It is of interest that the comparison of treatment and control groups for the study population as a whole by the beginning score level alone and then by social status level alone failed to reveal that the categories Family Relationships and Unity and Individual Behavior and Adjustment were areas in which the program had a positive impact. When, however, the comparison is made for levels of beginning functioning combined with levels of social status, these are found to be areas of living in which the treatment program was moderately effective for certain of the families at least.

Social Activities and Use of Community Resources represent the only two categories in which the findings depart from the pattern noted above. In the case of the former category the treatment cases registered more positive movement than the control cases, while the treatment cases showed slightly more negative movement in the latter category.

Other social status/beginning score levels. In families comprising the remaining categories of combined social status and beginning functioning, differences in movement between treatment and control groups were found to be minimal for most categories of functioning and for total score. It was not possible to make the comparisons between treatment and control cases for certain levels of social class and beginning functioning combinations for the numbers of treatment and/or control families falling into these categories were too small to permit meaningful comparisons. This was frequently the case at each class level with families having low beginning scores.

Summary. The data presented above tend to support the contention that the program of intervention proved highly successful with regard to one of its major goals, the prevention of malfunctioning for certain Class VI families which were functioning adequately at the start of the Project and, to a lesser extent, Class V families at a similar level of beginning functioning. It is evident that, of these families, those which did not receive the support and help offered by the FLIP Program were more likely to move toward problematic functioning. The findings suggest that the social context of the life situation for families at the lowest social stratum--amount of income, adequacy of housing, job satisfaction, etc.--makes for potential malfunctioning, which is more apt to be prevented when services are given to those showing some initial strength in social functioning.

D.   ETHNICITY and the Impact of the Program

Another line of inquiry pursued by the researchers concerned the program's differential impact upon families of dissimilar racial backgrounds.   The analysis was necessarily restricted to Negro and white families because the study sample contained only a very small proportion of families of other racial or ethnic backgrounds.

The question of race and its effect on living patterns has long been the subject of considerable discussion (and little research) by professionals in the behavioral sciences.   In 1965 with the release of the government report The Negro Family - The Case for National Action, better known as the Moynihan Report after its chief author, Daniel Patrick Moynihan, the issue became particularly controversial and heated. In a recent report, "Social Class, Ethnicity, and Family Functioning," two of the authors of this manuscript examined the relationship between race and social class and family functioning, concluding that social status, not race, is the predominant factor affecting the quality of family functioning[13]

Oscar Lewis[14] in his discussions of the culture of poverty identifies the lower-class Negro as belonging to that culture and exhibiting, along with other members, certain behavioral and attitudinal adaptations which tend to manifest themselves in family malfunctioning and a resistance to help from social agencies.

Wishing to examine the possible effect of race on service outcome, we compared differences in the movement of treatment and control cases for whites and blacks.   Since class and race are highly correlated and the objective was to focus upon race itself, we compared the differences in the movement of treatment and control cases for whites and blacks within each social class level.[15]   As in the previous analysis three levels of social status were employed.

Briefly, we found that the FLIP program of intervention was slightly more successful with Negro than with white families at each of the three levels of social status.

Black and white families of Class I-IV.   Before presenting the results, we must caution the reader to regard the findings as highly tentative for they are based on a relatively small number of Class I-IV Negro families (eight in the treatment group and twelve in the control group).

Overall movement scores suggest that Negro families at the highest level of social status were helped by the program of services to a slightly greater degree than white families of a similar social status. For Negro families the relationship between inclusion in the treatment group rather than the control group and subsequent shifts in total score is reflected in a gamma of +.375, whereas for white families no such relationship was observed, the gamma being equal to zero.

When the comparison is made for each area of functioning, both black and white families of this high social status who had received services did better in five of the eight areas than those who had not. For black families of this status level, experimental/control group differences exceeded a minimal magnitude in two areas, Use of Community Resources and Economic Conditions and Practices. For higher social status white families, the experimental/control group differences were most pronounced in the area of Social Activities. It should be noted that for both black and white families of this social status there was one area each in which having received services tended to be correlated with deterioration. For blacks the area of deterioration was Family Relationships and Unity while for whites it was Use of Community Resources.

The areas and gammas obtained are presented below:

Category	Black Families Class I-IV (N=20) Gamma	White Families Class I-IV (N=35) Gamma
Family Relationships & Unity	-.322	
Social Activities		+.375
Economic Practices	+.400	
Use of Community Resources	+.412	-1.00

Black and white families of Class V.   Comparison of the overall movement scores showed that the program of intervention was slightly more effective for black than for white families of this social class.   The relationship between inclusion in the treatment or control group and total score movement is +.239 for Negro families and +.099 for white families.

A similar picture of greater effectiveness for black families emerges when movement in the eight categories of functioning is considered.   Among Class V white families, treatment cases did at least minimally better in six of the eight areas than did control cases.   Among black families, treatment cases did better than control families in all of the eight areas.   For white families there were three categories and for black families two categories in which the gains of the treatment group relative to those of the control group exceeded a minimal magnitude (gamma $\geq +.3$ and/or chi square probability $\leq .05$).

The areas of greatest improvement as a result of services for white families were Care and Training of Children, Economic Practices, and Use of Community Resources, while for black families the areas were Social Activities and Health Conditions and Practices.   Gammas and chi square probabilities for the areas discussed are shown below:

Category	Black families Class V (N=86)		White families Class V (N=57)	
	Gamma	Chi Square Prob. Level	Gamma	Chi Square Prob. Level
Care/Training of Children			+.409	p<.20,2 d.f.
Economic Practices			+.333	p<.50,2 d.f.
Use of Community Resources			+.408	p<.50,2 d.f.
Social Activities	+.325	p<.20,2 d.f.		
Health Conditions & Practices	+.239	p<.01,2 d.f.		

Class VI families. Before presenting the data pertaining to Class VI families, it should be pointed out that the significance of this analysis is severely restricted for only 14 white families, 10 treatment and 4 control, are included in this subsample.

The findings, however, exhibit a consistent pattern of changes in total scores and movement in the component areas of family functioning so that despite the exceedingly small number of families on which the data are based, they merit presentation here. The data suggest that white families of this class respond negatively to the program of intervention, whereas black families, although not registering positive change as a result of the service program, do not appear to be adversely affected.

Among white families of Class VI the treatment group showed considerably more deterioration than the control group in overall movement and in six of the eight areas of family functioning. In only two areas, Economic Practices and Home and Household Practices, did the treatment group exhibit a positive edge over the control group, and these differences were minimal.

The strength of the relationship between having been in the treatment group and negative movement for white families is evidenced by fairly high gammas. (Four of the six gammas were greater than -.50 and the remaining two were equal to -.33 and -.39.)

Among black families of Class VI the treatment group did slightly better than the control group in total scores and in four areas of functioning. In the four remaining areas, however, the treatment families did slightly more poorly than the control group. The differences between the control and treatment groups, in either a positive or negative direction, were not statistically significant and of an exceedingly small magnitude. Five of the gammas obtained fall below ±.100 and none exceed ±.260. It is evident that the service program was less helpful to black families in Class VI than to those in Classes I-IV and V.

Summary. The data presented in Summary Chart D reveal that at each of the three levels of social status treatment for the most part was more likely to result in small but positive changes in functioning for black families than it was for white families.

Summary Chart D

	Social Class I-IV Black families	Social Class I-IV White families	Social Class V Black families	Social Class V White families	Social Class VI Black families	Social Class VI White families
a. Treatment group made greater gains than control group on total score	Yes	No	Yes	Yes	Yes	No (control group did better)
b. Was the difference, if any, in total score considerable (chi square $p \leq .05$ and/or gamma $\geq +.3$)?	Yes	–	No	No	No	Yes
c. Number of areas in which treatment group did better than control group	5	5	8	6	4	2
d. Number of areas in which treatment group did considerably better (chi square $p \leq .05$ and/or gamma $\geq +.3$)	2	1	2	3	0	0
e. Number of areas in which treatment group did more poorly than control group	3	3	0	2	4	6
f. Number of areas in which treatment group did considerably more poorly (chi square $p \leq .05$ and/or gamma $\geq -.3$)	1	1	–	0	0	6

Among families in Class I-IV participation in treatment benefited black families more than white families with regard to overall positive movement.   This same difference was observed for families of Class V.   In addition, among the latter families the number of areas in which the treatment group showed more positive movement was slightly greater for black than for white families.   As to Class VI families, the difference between the races was of a different nature.   Treatment made very little difference for black families in this Class, and in fact, compared with the movement of black families at the higher status levels, the gains were even smaller.   Here the contrast with white families of the same class lies in the fact that the latter were not even minimally helped.   In point of fact, the functioning of white families of this class level seemed to be negatively affected by exposure to services.

Needless to say the Class VI findings should be viewed as tentative since they are based on a very small number of families.

E.   MARITAL STATUS and Effectiveness of Treatment[16]

A further avenue of exploration lay in the assessment of the treatment program's relative effectiveness for families headed by married parents and unmarried mothers.

Underlying this line of inquiry were two contradictory expectations: the first, that services would profit one-parent families to a lesser extent than two-parent families;   and the other, the reverse.   Lewis[17] cites a high prevalence of illegitimacy as a characteristic of the culture of poverty.   Inasmuch as most of the unmarried mothers (90 out of 114 or 79%) fell into Class VI, it seemed highly likely that most of these families belonged to the poverty culture and as such might be expected to respond negatively to efforts of help.   On the other hand, common sense suggests that the burden of bearing the sole responsibility for the family--earning an income, caring for one or more children, running a household, and coping with the multitude of problems that arise in the course of living--would tend to make unmarried mothers and their families more receptive to help than married parents.

The data suggest that perhaps both these forces were operating and cancelled each other out, since the helpfulness of the program was approximately equivalent for both married and unmarried clients.   If we examine the differences in total score movement between the treatment and control families headed by unmarried mothers and those headed by married parents, we find that for both kinds of families the treatment group contains a higher proportion of clients for which the outcome was positive than the control group.   In both instances, however, the differences were small and not statistically significant.   (Gammas were equal to +.176 for the one-parent families and +.106 for the two-parent families.)

Focusing on the eight separate areas of family functioning, it is observed that among families headed by married parents the treatment group did at least minimally better than the control group in five categories while among families headed by an unmarried mother the treatment group did at least minimally better in six categories.   For each group of families the differences between treatment and control families were found to be statistically significant in one area, Care and Training of Children for families headed by unmarried mothers and Health Conditions and Practices for families headed by married parents.   Gammas and chi square probabilities for the two categories are shown below:

Category	Families headed by unmarried mothers Classes V & VI (N = 120)		Families headed by married parents Classes V & VI (N = 176)	
	Gamma	Chi Square Prob. Level	Gamma	Chi Square Prob. Level
Care & Training of Children	+.393	p<.05, 2 d.f.		
Health Conditions & Practices			+.032	p<.01, 2 d.f.

F.   FUNCTIONING OF FAMILY of Orientation
     and Effectiveness of Treatment

Two previous studies, one by Geismar[18] and the other by Kirkpatrick[19] have produced evidence of the fact that adequacy of functioning of a given family is related to the adequacy of the functioning of the families in which the parents grew up.   The question we are raising here is whether the functioning of the parental families is an intervening factor in the relationship between services and outcome. Is the impact of services upon a family affected at all by the functioning of the parents' own families of origin, whether they grew up in a household relatively free of severe difficulties or in a home beset by a multitude of serious problems? The question has been virtually ignored in the social work literature except for the attention that has been given to those families which themselves exhibit a high degree of malfunctioning and which are headed by mothers and fathers who grew up in similarly malfunctioning families.

The following analysis of the effects of functioning of the family of origin on the study family's functioning was limited to the mother's family because in a third of the study families information on the paternal side was missing.[20] Three levels of functioning of maternal family of origin were established: most adequate, moderately adequate, and least adequate. (The procedure for rating families of orientation is described in note 14 of Chapter 5.) When differences between treatment and control families are examined at each level of functioning of maternal family of orientation with regard to shifts in total scores and in categories of functioning, they were found to be minimal with one exception, suggesting that the maternal family's level of functioning does not materially influence the effectiveness of services. The exception was the category Care and Training of Children for families with mothers who grew up in moderately well-functioning families. (A gamma of $+.412$ was obtained and a chi square significant at a probability level of less than $.05$, 2 d.f., $N=112$.) When we refine the analysis still further, however, examining differences between treatment and control families not only by level of functioning of the mothers' family of orientation but by the study family's beginning level of functioning as well, we find that the program of intervention appears to have had maximum influence upon families in which the level of functioning of the mother's family was rated least adequate, but whose own beginning functioning was assessed as adequate. Family units in which the mother's family of orientation functioning at a moderately adequate level and whose own beginning scores were at an adequate level, also appeared to derive considerable benefit from the program of services but to a slightly lesser extent.

Families characterized by highest beginning scores and least adequate functioning of maternal family of orientation. Total score changes that occurred in this group of families were inconspicuous. Although the treatment group did register more positive movement than the control group, the difference was minimal and not statistically significant. This is reflected in a gamma of +.026.

The area by area analysis reveals that those families which had been in the treatment group made greater gains in six out of eight areas of functioning than those in the control group. This includes all categories of functioning except for Social Activities and the Use of Community Resources. The differences were significant in five of the six areas mentioned above. Gammas and chi square probability levels for the six areas are shown below:

Category	Gamma	Chi Square Probability Level	Total Number Cases
Family Relation- ships & Unity	+.607	p<.05, 1 d.f.	42
Individual Behavior	+.793	p<.01, 1 d.f.	31
Care/Training of Children	+.628	p<.02, 1 d.f.	54
Economic Practices	+.760	p=.03, 1 d.f. *	26
Home & House- hold Practices	+.333	p<.50, 1 d.f.	28
Health Condi- tions/Practices	+.716	p<.02, 1 d.f.	31

*Fisher's Exact Test was used because of small total number of cases.

Families characterized by highest beginning scores and moderately adequate functioning of maternal family of orientation. Among these families, treatment and control cases differed with regard to total score changes, the treatment group manifesting relatively more positive movement than the control group. A gamma of +.400 and a chi square probability level less than .30 (2 d.f.; N=46) was obtained, the latter figure falling below the level of statistical significance.

The area by area analysis reveals relatively more positive change on the part of the treatment group compared with the control group in five of the eight categories. The differences noted between the two groups were of a moderate to fairly high magnitude, with significant differences found in two areas. Gammas and chi square probability levels obtained with respect to the five areas discussed are presented below:

Category	Gamma	Chi Square Probability Level	Total Number Cases
Care/Training of Children	+.448	$p < .05$, 1 d.f.	73
Social Activities	+.500	$p < .10$, 1 d.f.	50
Economic Practices	+.300	$p < .50$, 1 d.f.	52
Home & House-hold Practices	+.342	$p < .30$, 1 d.f.	46
Health Conditions & Practices	+.636	$p < .05$, 1 d.f.	41

Families with lowest beginning scores and least adequate functioning of maternal family of orientation. Particular attention was directed toward these families. They came closest to fitting the designation "multi-problem families", malfunctioning units in which at least one parent grew up in a family also characterized by considerable deprivation and disorganization. The evidence, albeit meager, suggests that the program of intervention was beneficial to a limited extent.

In total scores, the treatment group manifested slightly greater but not significant gains when compared with the control group. This is reflected in a gamma of +.185.

In categories of functioning, the treatment group improved to a greater extent than the control group in four of the eight categories. In two categories the treatment group performed either more poorly or about as well as the control group, and in the two remaining categories the sample size was too small to permit a meaningful analysis.

In the four areas in which the treatment group registered more positive movement than the control group the differences with regard to relative movement were small in one
area and of moderate magnitude in the other three. The three
categories are listed below with the appropriate gammas obtained. Chi squares were not computed because of the small
sample size. *

Category	Gamma	Total Number Families
Care & Training of Children	+.548	15
Economic Practices	+.333	28
Health Conditions & Practices	+.529	20

*These were 2 x 3 tables; therefore, the Fisher's Exact
Test, appropriate only for 2 x 2 tables, could not be used.

Other levels of beginning score and functioning of maternal family of orientation. For the families which made up
the remaining combined levels of beginning score and functioning of maternal family of orientation, no meaningful pattern of differences in movement between treatment and control groups were found. Two of the sub-samples among families registering low beginning scores, one characterized by
most adequate functioning and the other by moderately adequate functioning of maternal family of orientation, contained
too few cases for meaningful analysis.

Summary. The analysis of levels of functioning of the
mother's family of orientation failed to reveal differences with
regard to the impact of the program. However, when functioning of the maternal family of orientation was combined with
beginning level of functioning of the study family a particularly
interesting set of findings emerged. Of all the groups comprising the various possible combinations, those families for
whom the program of intervention had the most positive effect
were the ones in which the mother grew up in a highly malfunctioning family but which themselves were functioning at an
adequate level at the start of the study. Among this group of
families the experimental cases showed considerably greater
gains than the control group in all but two categories of functioning.

Another group of families for whom the program had a highly positive effect was that in which the mother's family of orientation had functioned at a moderately adequate level but which themselves functioned at the most adequate level at the beginning of the study. The effect of services was somewhat less marked for these families than for the former group of families.

Finally, families in which both their own functioning at the outset of the project and that of the maternal family of orientation were at the most problematic level seemed to derive only limited benefit from the treatment program.

The findings reported above suggest, first of all, that malfunctioning of family of origin under certain circumstances does, in fact, affect the relationship between receiving services and outcome. Specifically, inadequate functioning of maternal family of origin resulted in a more positive response to service for families who themselves were functioning adequately at the outset of the study. The findings also suggest that those families which most closely resemble the hard to reach and hard to help "multi-problem" families described in the literature did profit, though to a limited extent, from the services offered by FLIP.

Summary and Interpretation of Findings

Briefly reviewing the foregoing, we found that in considering the sample as a whole, the families in the treatment group compared with those in the control group did not show significantly more improvement in total score changes. They did show significantly more improvement in three of eight separate categories of family functioning, namely, Care and Training of Children, Home and Household Practices, and Health Conditions and Practices.

The results of the analysis holding problemicity constant suggest that services were most beneficial for families which at the outset of the study were functioning at the highest and lowest levels; the program was least profitable for those families whose beginning scores fell into the middle range.

When comparing the outcome of treatment and control groups by social class, families in Classes V and VI appeared to derive slightly greater benefit as a result of service than those in social Classes I-IV.

Further refinement of the analysis by social class and beginning score revealed that the program of intervention was of maximum effectiveness for Class VI families which, at the start of the study, were functioning at an adequate level.

Examination of the relationship between ethnicity and effectiveness of services revealed that black families in social Classes I-IV and V were helped to a slightly greater extent than white families in the same classes. The most striking differences between black and white families emerged in Class VI. The impact of the treatment program appeared to be negative for white families while it was, although minimal, predominantly positive for Negroes.

When examining the effect of marital status on treatment, it was found that services had an equivalent impact on families headed by either an unmarried mother or married parents.

When level of functioning of the mother's family of orientation was introduced into the analysis by itself, it seemed to make little difference in terms of the effectiveness of services. However, when functioning of the maternal family of orientation was combined with the family's own beginning level of functioning, it was found that units registering the greatest gains were those in which the mother grew up in a highly malfunctioning family but which themselves were functioning at an adequate level at the onset of the study (which was also the start of the family life cycle). The next most likely to benefit were families in which the mother's family of orientation had functioned at a moderately adequate level and whose own beginning functioning was at the most adequate level. Families with mothers who grew up in highly problematic families and which themselves exhibited a relatively high degree of problemicity at the beginning of the project showed improvement in certain areas as a result of treatment.

For the most part, the data emerging as a result of the analysis of sub-groups reveals that groups of families occupying a marginal position in society fared at least as well and sometimes better at the end of treatment compared with those whose positions are in the so-called mainstream of American life.

The comparisons, which had covered the sample as a whole as well as 35 sub-groups, showed that the program of intervention was consistently effective for Class VI families

functioning at an adequate level at the start of the study and
for families which themselves evidenced no malfunctioning at
the project's beginning but in which the mother's family or
orientation had been evaluated as highly problematic.   It is
of interest that the program of services proved most effective
with non-problematic families in which a latent factor tending
toward malfunctioning was potentially present.   In one instance,
the latent factor consists of the ∘Class VI social milieu, in
which the realization of many family and personal goals and
aspirations of both an expressive and instrumental nature is
frequently blocked.   In the other instance, the latent factor
consists of the total effect that growing up in a malfunctioning
family has upon the individual's personality, his relationships
with others, his way of coping with problems, etc.   The data
leaves little doubt that, as far as the above families are concerned, those which did not receive the support provided by
the program of intervention showed considerably more deterioration than the families which received FLIP help.

The group of families most negatively affected by the
FLIP program were white families of Class VI, but no explanation of this finding is provided by the data.   We can
merely speculate that in some way the FLIP service program
interfered with the normal or usual sources of support, or
that perhaps the relative deprivation experienced by whites
of this social class is so great that it results in a highly
negative response to service.

Turning to the areas of effectiveness, it is possible
to identify categories of greatest and least effectiveness by
simply counting for the 35 sub-samples the total number of
times in each area that the treatment group was considerably
more positive than the control group or the reverse was
true. [21]   For each category the total number of sub-samples
in which the program had a positive or a negative effect is
given below.   Those areas in which the treatment families
did significantly better than the control families for the sample as a whole are marked by an asterisk.

Care and Training of Children and Health Conditions
and Practices emerge as the two areas in which the Family
Life Improvement Project had the greatest impact.   These
are followed by three additional areas--Home and Household
Practices, Social Activities, and Economic Practices.   The
first three are areas of effectiveness for the sample as a
whole as well as for a number of sub-samples;   the last two
did not emerge as areas of effectiveness for the sample as
a whole but for several sub-samples only.

Category	Total number of Sub-samples for which program had a positive effect	Total number of Sub-samples for which program had a negative effect
*Care & Training of Children	14	1
*Health Conditions & Practices	9	1
Economic Practices	8	0
Social Activities	7	1
*Home & Household Practices	5	1
Individual Behavior & Adjustment	4	2
Family Relationships & Unity	2	2
Community Resources	2	6

Areas in which the program was relatively ineffective were Individual Behavior and Adjustment, Family Relationships and Unity, and Use of Community Resources. The failure of the program to aid Project participants in the use of Community Resources is signified not only by the relatively small number of sub-groups in which the treatment group did better but also by the fact that the number of sub-samples in which the control families did better than the treatment families exceeded the number in all other categories.

The eight areas of family living can be subsumed under three more general aspects of functioning: (1) expressive areas, having to do with intra- and extra-familial relationships; (2) instrumental areas, covering the maintenance of the physical system and pertaining to the means rather than the goals of family life; and (3) role behavior areas, comprising individual behavior in and adjustment to a variety of social situations. An examination of these reveals that the instrumental areas showed the greatest degree of success,

for three of the five areas in which the program proved to
be most effective, Health, Household Practices, and Economic Practices, are instrumental in nature. A fourth category,
Care and Training of Children, is also instrumental in character to a large extent, although certain expressive components are present. Social Activities emerges as the one expressive area in which the FLIP worker was effective for
certain groups of families. The findings are consistent with
other outcome studies which show that social work's greatest
gains fall within the areas of instrumental functioning (for
further discussion see Chapter 9 of this book).

On the whole, the program failed to improve functioning in the expressive and role behavior areas of Family Relationships and Unity, and Individual Behavior and Adjustment.
The lack of success in these intra- and interpersonal areas
is also in accord with the results of other social work outcome studies.

The relatively high measure of success in the areas
of instrumental functioning (the program proved to be moderately to very successful in all but one instrumental category)
and the relatively high degree of failure in the expressive
and role behavior areas is, in all probability, related to the
nature of the problems and solutions characterizing the two
facets of functioning. To a large extent worker effectiveness
in any given area depends upon the ease with which problems
can be identified, evidence that the means employed to cope
with these problems really work, and the availability of tools
for change--appropriate skills, knowledge, resources--to the
worker. Problems relating to the instrumental area of functioning are usually of a concrete nature and as such readily
identifiable. By the same token, means of coping are generally clear-cut, and directly related to the problem itself. Thus,
provided that the appropriate resources and facilities are available, the worker can be effective. A family member with a
health problem can be taken to a clinic or private physician;
a family in need of more adequate housing can be helped to
find such housing; a mother can be advised as to the appropriate diet for an infant. On the other hand, problems related to functioning in role behavior and the expressive area
are of quite a different nature. Identification of the problem
is sometimes difficult, depending to a large extent on the professional background and orientation of the diagnostician. Then
again professional opinion differs regarding the techniques of
coping with many of the problems. In short, many of the
difficulties which are of an intra- and interpersonal nature

fall within fields of knowledge made up of competing and frequently untested psycho-social theories.

Perhaps the most disappointing finding which emerged
from the study was FLIP's obvious failure to promote the use
of community resources. As pointed out previously, this was
the one instrumental area in which the project did not have at
least a moderate degree of success. Indeed, there is evidence that, for certain groups of families, the existence of
services resulted in more malfunctioning in this area than its
absence. This was unanticipated, for one of the major goals
of the project had been the education of clients in the use of
needed resources. Furthermore, other studies which had
identified this component of helping showed it to be an area
of substantial success. The answer probably lies in the relationship between service efforts and available resources. [22]
Service projects such as FLIP can have only a limited effect
upon the ways in which local agencies and institutions serve
their populations. At best, the projects carry out a measure
of resource coordination, help clients communicate with them,
and play an advocacy role. Two factors are likely to enter
into a favorable outcome: The quality and potential respon-
siveness of community agencies, and the prestige and power
enjoyed by the service project. On both counts the Family
Life Improvement Project compared unfavorably with the two
other programs (Vancouver ADP and New Haven NIP) where
a systematic study of the use of community resources was
undertaken. The service structure within which FLIP operated was less adequate in relation to local need and more im-
pervious to pressures for reform than those within which the
other two programs were established.

Longitudinal change patterns of treatment and control
cases. Still another way in which the effect of intervention
might be assessed is through a comparative analysis of change
patterns in treatment and control families. Because most
Project families had multiple evaluations of their social functioning, it was possible to chart a longitudinal functioning pattern for the whole study period. [23]

For purposes of the present report, we shall briefly
sketch and categorize the change patterns and furnish the percentage distribution of families in each category. There were
essentially three basic types of changes which characterized
study families, and we shall present the typology by attaching
labels to the family groups rather than to their behavior. The
three most basic types were: (A.) Straight liners, (B.) Steady

changers, and (C.) Zigzaggers. Straight liners did not change their mean level of family functioning or, if they did, modified it very little. Steady changers moved consistently either in an up or down direction, and zigzaggers showed an erratic pattern of up-and-down movement.

Each one of the basic types is subdivided into two or three sub-types and these are presented together with a more operational definition of change patterns.

A. Straight liners = change between the first and last evaluation is less than 4 scale points

   I. No changers = families whose family functioning scores are equal throughout or fluctuated within one scale point

   II. Hoverers = families whose scores are between 2 and 3 points apart

B. Steady changers = change is 4 or more scale points in one direction

   III. Climbers = families whose scores rise from beginning to end (allowing for one deviation from this trend)

   IV. Skidders = families whose scores fall from beginning to end (allowing for one deviation from this trend)

C. Zigzaggers = change is 4 or more scale points but of a fluctuating nature

   V. Zigzaggers-up = families whose scores end more than one point higher than the beginning position

   VI. Zigzaggers-even = families whose scores end at the same level as or within a point of the beginning position.

   VII. Zigzaggers-down = families whose scores end more than one point lower than the beginning position

The percentage distribution of families in the treatment and control groups according to the foregoing typology is given below:

			Treatment Group (N=177)	Control Group (N=137)
Straight	I.	No Changers	12.9%	8.8%
liners	II.	Hoverers	16.4	21.2
Steady	III.	Climbers	19.8	14.6
changers	IV.	Skidders	13.6	22.6
	V.	Zigzaggers-up	11.3	10.2
Zigzaggers	VI.	Zigzaggers-even	10.2	12.4
	VII.	Zigzaggers-down	15.8	10.2
	Total		100.0	100.0

$$x^2 = 8.09, \; 6 \; d.f., \; p<.30$$

We observe, first of all, that the three basic change groups are nearly equal in size, with the zigzaggers slightly in the lead. They constitute 35.4% of the combined treatment and control group and are divided almost equally into those going up, those staying even, and those going down during a two to three-year period. If the time of observation had been extended these families might have been located in a different terminal position, although they would still have been classified as zigzaggers. The next largest group are the steady changers, comprising 35.0% of study families. They, too, break evenly into families showing a steady improvement and families manifesting a steady deterioration during the period of the research action project. The third among the basic change types are the straightliners, who are only slightly less numerous than the two previous groups and constitute 29.6% of the research families. Among the straightliners there are more hoverers (changing their average social functioning by 2 to 3 points) than true steadies who do not change at all. The maintenance of a very even level of family functioning is a characteristic possessed by only eleven percent of our study families, but as a pattern of longitudinal functioning it is no less common than each one of the three types of zigzagging behavior.

Comparing treatment and control group families, we are struck by the dominant picture of similarity that emerges rather than basic difference between the two, an impression that is verified by the chi square test which yields a coefficient of 8.09 that is not statistically significant at six degrees of freedom. This finding supports the earlier observation we made on change patterns, in which we saw that the sum total of all kinds of influences upon family life overshadowed the effect of the kind of professional intervention the Family Life Improvement Project provided.

Nonetheless, as we turn our attention to the differences between treatment and control families in the specific change categories, we find that in one sector of the basic typology, the steady changers, differences are observed. Climbers are more strongly represented in the treatment group (by 5.2%) and skidders occur with greater frequency among the control cases (by 9.0%). These differences are statistically significant at less than the 5% level (X^2 = 5.26, 1 d.f.), suggesting that this is an area where the program of intervention may have been instrumental in modifying the longitudinal patterns of social functioning. Project influence, the analysis suggests, was somewhat greater in preventing families from skidding toward malfunctioning than in helping them climb toward adequate functioning.

To this point the focus has been largely on the differences between the treatment and control groups with respect to changes in family functioning. It is in no way our intention to obscure the fact that at the end of the treatment period the experimental and control groups were still more alike than different in social functioning and in the paths by which they reached their levels of functioning. Both groups were presumably reacting to the same kind of internal (biological, psychological, and intrafamilial social) and external (economic, political, and extrafamilial social) forces, which tended to shape their development in similar ways. However, in assessing this type of program's success the severe handicaps under which it operates must be taken into account. As pointed out earlier, the Family Life Improvement Program had little power to affect the performance of the social agencies and institutions serving the city. A worker might assist a client in obtaining the maximum grant allowance under the current public welfare system but was powerless vis-à-vis the fact that the largest grant provided the most minimal level of support for the family. Similarly, a FLIP worker might help a client find the best low-cost housing available in the city at that time but could not change the basic inadequacy of this housing.

The question of what we should realistically expect from a program of professional intervention given these limitations must be raised although it cannot readily be answered. Our data would indicate that professional intervention did have a small but measurable positive impact upon the life of the study families. Is this degree of impact sufficient to justify the kind of services offered, or are the services to be rejected unless more positive outcome can be demonstrated? We shall return to this question in the final chapter after an analysis of service patterns and an extension of the means of evaluation.

Notes

1. We wish to call the reader's attention to the fact that the research design called for four control sub-groups: (1) three times a year (2) twice a year (3) once a year and (4) before-after. Moreover, the study used still another control group of the "after only" type. A large attrition rate in the latter precluded our using it in the study. A comparison of change for total and area scores among each of the control sub-groups showed, with one exception, no significant differences. See Appendix C.

2. Matilda White Riley, Sociological Research II, New York: Harcourt, Brace & World, 1963, pp. 141-143.

3. Hubert M. Blalock, Social Statistics, McGraw-Hill, 1960 pp. 212-221.

4. Although the chi square obtained does not permit the rejection of the null hypothesis that the more positive movement of treatment families was due to chance, the more powerful t-test applied to the differences between mean movement scores of the two groups does show that the experimental group did significantly better. The means obtained for experimental and control groups were 30.19 and 28.98, respectively. The t obtained was 1.86, significant at .05 level. Appropriateness of use of t-test is a matter of controversy among statisticians. We opted for the more conservative nonparametric chi square.

5. The existence of statistically significant differences on some area scores vis-à-vis the nonsignificant differences on total score can be explained by a compensatory

effect resulting from some relationships of a low order counterbalancing those that are significant.

6. Norman Q. Brill and Hugh A. Sterrow, "Social Class
    and Psychiatric Treatment," in Frank Riessman,
    Jerome Cohen, Arthur Pearl (eds.), Mental Health
    of the Poor, New York: Free Press, 1964, pp. 68-
    75. Jules V. Coleman, Ruth Janowicz, Stephen
    Fleck, and Nea Norton, "A Comparative Study of a
    Psychiatric Clinic and a Family Agency, Part II,"
    Social Casework, Vol. 38, 2, February 1957, pp. 74-
    80. David Fanshel, "A Study of Caseworkers' Per-
    ceptions of Their Client," Social Casework, Vol. 39,
    10, December 1958, pp. 543-551. August B. Hollings-
    head and Frederick C. Redlich, Social Class and Men-
    tal Illness, New York: John Wiley, 1958, pp. 335-
    356. Henry Maas, "The Differential Use and Outcome
    of Childrens' Psychiatric Clinic Services," Smith Col-
    lege Studies in Social Work, Vol. 25, 2, February
    1955. H. Aaronson and Betty Overall, "Treatment
    Expectations in two Social Classes," Social Work,
    January 1966, pp. 35-41, Vol. II, 1. John E. Mayer
    and Noel Timms, "Clash in Perspective between Wor-
    ker and Client," Social Casework, Vol. 50, 1, Janu-
    ary 1969, pp. 32-40. David C. Speer, Merle Fossum,
    Hyman S. Lippman, Rene Schwartz, and Beth Slocum,
    "A Comparison of Middle- and Lower-Class Families
    in Treatment at a Child Guidance Clinic," American
    Journal of Orthopsychiatry, Vol. 38, 5, October 1968,
    pp. 814-822.

7. Mayer and Timms, loc. cit., p. 39.

8. State Charities Aid Association, "Multi-Problem Famil-
    ies" A New Name or a New Problem?, New York:
    Social Research Service, State Charities Aid Asso-
    ciation, May 1960.

9. Oscar Lewis, "The Culture of Poverty," Scientific Amer-
    ican, October 1966, Vol. 215, 4, pp. 19-24.

10. Ibid.

11.

Level of Beginning Functioning	Total Score	Main Category Score
Most adequate	53-56	7
Moderately adequate	47-52	5-6
Least adequate	46 or below	4 or less

12. For Total movement, total beginning scores were held constant; for area scores movement, beginning scores for each area examined were held constant.

13. Geismar and Gerhart, "Social Class, Ethnicity, and Family Functioning," loc. cit.

14. Lewis, op. cit., pp. 19-24.

15. In findings pertaining to Class I-IV Negro families and Class VI white families, the total number of cases was too small to permit the use of the chi square test of statistical significance. Furthermore, substitute measures, such as the Fisher's Exact Test which is appropriate for 2 x 2 tables, were not applicable because the three categories of movement cannot be meaningfully collapsed.

16. The analysis was limited to Classes V and VI only, since all but four unmarried mothers fell into these social classes.

17. Lewis, op. cit., p. 23.

18. Geismar, Preventive Intervention in Social Work, op. cit., pp. 43-46.

19. Kirkpatrick, "Measuring Marital Adjustment," loc. cit.

20. Data on the paternal families were often missing because the mother, the principal source of information, might have had little or no knowledge about her in-laws. She may not have known them and/or the father may not have provided her with much information about his family background.

21. The treatment was assessed to be considerably more positive in its effect when a chi square significant at the .05 probability level or less and/or gamma equal to or greater than +.3 was obtained. The treatment was regarded as considerably more negative when a chi square significant at the .05 level or less and/or a gamma equal to or greater than -.3 was obtained.

22. The gaps between social needs and resources are documented in George Sternlieb with Mildred Barry,

Social Needs and Social Resources - Newark 1967,
Newark, N. J. : Rutgers University Graduate School
of Business Administration, 1967.

23.   Before-and-after control cases were excluded in this
       analysis because they had fewer than three measure-
       ments.   As a result, the comparison is confined to
       177 treatment and 137 control group families, nearly
       all of which had between four and ten cross-sectional
       evaluations of their functioning.   The exceptions were
       three control cases which had only three evaluations.

Chapter 7

PATTERNS OF PROFESSIONAL INTERVENTION

Introduction and Overview

The program of intervention which we developed in the Family Life Improvement Project was based upon the proposition that professional intervention by social workers can have a positive effect upon the social functioning of young families. Professional intervention was viewed as service rendered by professionals with previous training and/or experience, working as paid employees under the direction of professionally trained, experienced supervisors within the framework of agency structure and objectives. We had originally planned to explore the relative effectiveness of professionally trained versus untrained social workers, but budget limitations prevented such a comparison. [1]

The reader will recall that in Chapter 2 we defined positive effect on social functioning as relative rather than absolute change. That is, we looked only for significantly more adequate functioning among families in the treatment group than in the control group even if this meant significantly less deterioration in the situation rather than measurable gain. The findings presented in Chapter 6 revealed that the program of intervention had a positive albeit limited effect upon the functioning of families, and thus a closer look at the nature of the services given to the families in the experimental group is in order.

As you may recall from Chapters 1 and 2 the type of program the Project had planned to offer and the kind of population it was to serve--a group of normal, young urban families--made it necessary to approach the question of services in a wholly pragmatic manner. There is neither literature nor informally collected practice wisdom on preventive services to young families. The intervention began with the assumption that in the 1960's young families needed help in coping with many of the daily problems of urban living. Because

such a service does not now exist in the United States--as it
does in some other countries--we decided to bring it to the
families by reaching out to them in their homes. Service
giving was to stem from a study of the family situation and
from assessment of their psycho-social functioning prior to
the start of the social action program. Thus, the program
of intervention was to be based upon the identification of levels
of social functioning for the specific family.[2]

Although this approach deals minimally with the theoretical and organizational supports which might be needed in
treatment, it has the advantage of leaving the treatment organization free to respond to client need unencumbered by a-
gency tradition or well established, yet untested practices. It
was hoped that a treatment program sharply focused on client
need could be evolved through an ongoing in-service training
program and through continuous and close supervision of workers by the treatment director and the two treatment supervisors who headed the service staff. Both techniques would
make use of the continuous feedback of information from practitioners on their day-by-day treatment experience. Frequency
of contact and treatment modalities would be determined largely by the families' own need.

The eight workers making up the service field staff
were college graduates; one of them had completed a master's
degree in educational counselling and was a candidate for the
doctor's degree. Half of the direct service staff, four workers, had been with public welfare prior to joining FLIP;
three had other forms of social work experience; and one had
only limited experience as a volunteer worker in planned parenthood. While in the Project the eight workers were closely
supervised by two professionally trained and experienced caseworkers, and they participated in a bi-weekly in-service training seminar. A specially designed instrument, the Treatment
Log, was used to record contact between experimental group
families and Project workers. The Log is described in detail in a later section of this chapter.

The outcome study reported in the previous chapter used
measurements of change in family functioning spanning the period from the first interview to the last, and in this way, similar timing of the interviews for experimental and control cases
was made possible. For purposes of studying the process of
treatment, however, the first treatment contact rather than the
first interview was employed as a basis of measurement; this
arrangement was necessitated by the fact that the first treatment contact followed the first interview by a period of several

months. During this time services could not be extended to
the experimental group for the initial interviewing process was
being completed. Consequently, the treatment program did
not spread over the total measurement period but covered
roughly a fifth less.[3]

In the subsequent sections of this chapter we shall be
concerned with an examination at length of the salient features
of the FLIP program noted thus far--its highly flexible, empirically oriented, client-centered approach to preventive intervention. In the first section to follow, devoted to the characteristics of the population served, the demographic composition and beginning level of social functioning of the 177 families remaining in the treatment program throughout intervention will be reviewed. A problem typology will be introduced
to give the reader an initial impression of the emerging needs
of the population. The next section will recapitulate FLIP intervention,[4] noting the assumptions underlying the development
of general treatment plans, outlining several broad-gauged
strategies addressed to three distinct levels of family functioning, commenting on the roles and functions of the worker. The
third section will consider the research issues involved in op-
erationalizing intervention preparatory to its study. An approach to the study of worker-client activity as a process of
social exchange will be introduced. The Treatment Log, developed toward both practice and research ends, is described
with an accompanying schema for coding intervention records.
The fourth section deals with patterns of intervention and their
relationship to change in family functioning. In a final comment, an attempt is made to explicate the role of the social
worker and assess his effectiveness as it is related to techniques he employed in treatment.

Characteristics of the Population Served

Of the 272 families in the Family Life Improvement
Project treatment group, 177 remained in the treatment program throughout the study,[5] constituting the population served.
A comparison of these 177 families with the original 272 reveals that they are essentially alike in demographic characteristics and type of presenting problem, but that the group remaining in the treatment program contained a slightly higher
proportion of adequately functioning families. (See Appendix
E, Tables 1 and 2.)

Demographic characteristics. Relative to ethnicity, social class, and marital status, the population served resembled

the study population as a whole (see Chapter 4). Approximately two-thirds were Negro (62%), one quarter non-Spanish
speaking, native white (27%), and 11% Spanish speaking (mostly
Puerto Rican) and foreign born. Eighty-six percent of those
served were lower-class families (modified Hollingshead V
and VI), 13% middle-class (III and IV), and 1% upper-class
(I and II). Slightly over one-third (37%) of the families were
headed by an unwed mother. In line with the overall study
design, all mothers in the population served were under 30
years of age at the time of their first birth. The families
had only one child at the beginning of treatment.

Beginning family functioning scores. The distribution
of overall beginning family functioning scores for the clients
served is as follows: 36% obtained the highest scores ranging
from 59-63; 29% obtained the next highest scores of 54-58;
15% received ratings of 49-53; 12% scores of 44-48, and the
remaining 8% received scores of 43 and below, denoting least
adequate functioning. [6]

Problem Types. Elaboration of a major problem typology will aid both in giving an initial impression of the emerging needs of the population which was served and in the later
analysis of intervention patterns. According to our definition
a family presented a major problem whenever its profile of
family functioning contained a rating of 4 (marginal functioning) or less (below marginal, near inadequate, or inadequate
functioning) in one or more of the St. Paul Scale sub-categories.
Marginal functioning has already been defined as behavior marked by instability, conflict, deviancy from accepted norms,
inability to meet social, emotional and material needs--all of
these being of human and professional concern but not sufficiently severe to permit legally justifiable community intervention. Following the identification of such families, the
type of problem or problems was designated, whether in the
expressive, instrumental, or role areas of functioning. (For
definitions of the three areas of functioning see the previous
chapter.) The three problem types and the sub-categories of
family functioning comprising each are listed below:

PROBLEM TYPE   SUB-CATEGORY

Expressive   Marital Relationship, Parent-Child Re-
                                lationship, Sibling Relationship, Family
                                Solidarity, Relationship with Other
                                Household Members, Child Training
                                Methods, [7] Informal Social Activities,

Formal Social Activities, Attitude to-
wards the Worker, Use of Worker[8]

Instrumental   Physical Care of Children, Source and
                            Amount of Income, Job Situation, Use
                            of Money, Physical Facilities (home),
                            Housekeeping Standards, Health Condi-
                            tions, Health Practices, Use of the fol-
                            lowing community resources: School,
                            Church, Health, Social, and Recreation-
                            al Agencies

Role   Individual Behavior and Adjustment of
                            all family members considered individ-
                            ually

The population served presented the following constel-
lation or problems at the beginning of the service program:

PROBLEM TYPE	POPULATION SERVED (N=177)
Instrumental Only	17%
Instrumental-Expressive-Role	11%
Expressive Only	5%
Expressive-Role	4%
Instrumental-Expressive	3%
Instrumental-Role	3%
Role Only	--
No Major Problem	57%
	100%

Fifty-seven percent of the experimental group were
found to present no major problems; that is, their scores
in all areas were 5 or above.[9] Among the 43% who did present one or more major problems, 17% faced substantial problems in the instrumental area of functioning, the area related

to maintaining the family as a physical system through such
activities as income provision, housing, and physical child
care.   Eleven percent of the families revealed substantial
problems in all three areas--instrumental, expressive, and
role.   The expressive area of problemicity involved 5% of
the families served and the remaining 10% fell into various
combinations of two of the three problem areas.

   Interrelationships of social characteristics.   Negroes
were more likely than whites to present one or more major
problems (53% and 25%, respectively) and a higher proportion
were found in both of the problem-type categories most frequently observed, instrumental problems alone (20% of the
Negro families and 13% of the white families).   Frequencies
for the other problem-type categories were too small to merit
meaningful analysis.

   Compared to families headed by married parents, those
headed by unmarried mothers were more apt to exhibit one or
more major problems (72% compared to 26%).   Relatively more
unmarried than married parents were found who had only instrumental problems (30% compared to 10%) or instrumental-
expressive-role problems (21% against 5%).

   The relationship between social class and problemicity
formed a straight regression line as follows: Classes I-III:
15%;   Class IV: 23%;   Class V: 34%;   Class VI: 60%.   For
Class V families the heaviest concentration of problemicity
was in the instrumental areas (13%), while Class VI families
fell in the instrumental (30%) and instrumental-expressive-
role areas (16%).

   Summary of characteristics of the population served.
Before describing the program of services, it would be wise
to restate the characteristics of the target population.   Of
every ten families six were black, three were white, and one
was Spanish speaking.   Eighty-six percent of the families
were in Social Classes V and VI, 13% in Classes III and IV,
and only 1% in Social Classes I and II.   One in every three
families served was headed by an unwed mother.

   Fifty-seven percent of the families in the program could
be said to show no seriously problematic functioning.   When
we break down the remaining 43% into the three problem types
noted, we find that 17% of all families experienced instrumental problems, only 5% had expressive problems, 11% had a
combination of instrumental, expressive, and role problems,

and the remaining 10% were approximately evenly distributed among combinations of two of the three problem types.

Problemicity was twice as prevalent among blacks, and over two and a half times more prevalent among unmarried mothers. Sixty percent of Social Class VI families had problems, compared to 34% of Class V families, 23% of Class IV families, and 15% of the families in Social Classes I through III. Instrumental problems predominated among all the problematic groups noted, followed by the combined instrumental-expressive-role clustering of problems.

With this overall picture of population characteristics in mind, let us set forth the Project's strategy of intervention as a general backdrop against which to view the actual program of services.

The Intervention Strategy

As observed in the beginning of this chapter, the scarcity of information on preventive intervention with young urban families in the early 1960's made it necessary for the Family Life Improvement Project to design its program of intervention in a wholly pragmatic manner. More precisely, this meant that specification of service inputs would have to rest on a study of family situations and psycho-social functioning prior to the start of the social action program. Efforts along just these lines were made by Geismar in the early months of the Project and are spelled out in Preventive Intervention in Social Work.[10] The following section of this chapter will include a number of passages from this volume that are relevant here as a framework within which to view the subsequent extensive analysis of intervention patterns and their relationship to treatment outcome.

But first, let us make explicit two important assumptions which underlie any effort such as this to develop general treatment plans or intervention models. From the outset of work on strategies, there was an awareness of the fact that no one treatment plan could fit a great number of families-- to be effective it needs to be fitted to the diagnosis of each case. Yet a further assumption was made. In spite of the infinite variation among a large number of families, many share certain common characteristics, and these can be used to establish a collective treatment plan.

The first step in developing such a treatment plan, or model, is to enumerate the shared characteristics of young urban families.   Then, in keeping with accepted research procedures, the researcher must cast specific shared dimensions and their related characteristics into empirical types with relevance for treatment planning.   These types need not be completely uniform although they should show modal patterns of behavior along specified dimensions, which in this instance is family functioning.   Because the model does not envisage an individual fitting of case and intervention method but pertains rather to a collection of both, it is necessarily general;   it projects a strategy of intervention rather than tactics.

Several broad gauged strategies have been specified in the manner outlined above.   They relate to families functioning at three distinct levels as measured by the St. Paul Scale: The Adequate and Near Adequate level, the Near Problematic level, and the Problematic level. [11]

Intervention with adequate and near adequate families. At this level intervention programming cannot look for much guidance from the limited data about social malfunctioning. Families in the Adequate and Near Adequate categories are more likely to be from the higher socio-economic status groups, and such problems as they do encounter tend to be in the expressive or role behavior rather than the instrumental areas of functioning.

Adequate and Near Adequate families are usually able to recover from crises without intensive services.   Consequently, appropriate intervention is likely to take the form of information-giving and the offering of advice, steering the client toward resources offering limited counseling for behavior or relationship problems.   Essentially, service at this level means building upon existing family strengths in order to help members overcome disappointment, anxiety, and frustration; it may also mean effecting some modification in environmental conditions to relieve stress.   Education regarding the availability of resources in times of need would appear especially appropriate for these families.   On the whole, however, service here is on a stand-by basis, geared to respond with maximum flexibility to requests for help.

Preventive intervention with this group or any other group of families cannot limit itself to action based on the actual or projected problem profile.   Family functioning, and malfunctioning for that matter, does not take place in a sociocultural vacuum but occurs within the context of family hopes, aspirations, values, and life goals. The relationship between these goals and the family's actual opportunity to achieve them may become an important determinant, albeit not the only one, of the character of family functioning. Thus, preventive action must take cognizance of family values and aspirations and seek to encourage behavior which is in line with realistic goals. This means that the intervenor must be more than a trouble shooter; he must help the family identify and articulate life goals and examine ways to attain them. The conditions for achieving both satisfaction and goals are inherent in a family's psycho-social situation. That situation which comprises social, economic, biological, and psychological factors is not rigidly fixed but is in a state of flux as a result of the family's bio-social development and changes in the social structure. A program of prevention needs to address itself to the interplay of these forces within a perspective of family development.

To be Adequate or Near Adequate, a family must be well organized, must satisfactorily carry out its various socially expected tasks, and must be able to cope with daily problems. Adequate families like to believe that their own resources are sufficient for coping with their problems without help from the outside. [12] Such families, it may be assumed, are more future oriented than problem families simply because their coping skills have been developed as a result of situations which they anticipated and for which they prepared themselves.

Given this kind of orientation the emphasis in intervention ought to be upon an enhancement of social functioning. The primary approach would be educational rather than remedial[13] and would be inherently more positive and broader in conception than the public health concept of primary prevention which, after all, has as its referent specific diseases or pathologies. Largely neglected in the field of social work, prevention with an educational perspective must begin with the overall assumption that all family members have aspirations. It must then seek to identify these aspirations and to relate them to the developmental tasks facing the family and to the capacity of family members to carry out these tasks and realize their goals. The educational approach attempts to explore, with the family, new ways of gaining satisfactions through the acquisition of new knowledge and skills, particularly in the fields of recreation and culture; through the enhancement of social participation in the community; through the promotion of individual and collective self-expression appropriate to individual ability and need; and through a host of other techniques.

At the same time, the notion that the family is a system needing to guard itself against possible malfunctioning is
played down; instead, the theme of positive action in response
to family growth and development and ever changing life situation and needs is emphasized. From the point of view of prevention, such action may be likened to a process of generalized immunization rather than a technique using one special
serum for the prevention of a specific disease. Enhancement
of social functioning as defined here is no more than a broad
concept which requires translation into a variety of empirically developed techniques. The present social functioning
analysis is only a first step in this direction.

Intervention with near problematic families. Intervention with Near Problematic families must be planned with their
specific characteristics in mind, namely, the problems they are
likely to reveal in the intra- and interpersonal areas and in
instrumental behavior as well. By and large, the well-being
of family members is not seriously impaired and stresses on
family life are apt to be moderate. Family members have
adaptive skills and/or access to some resources which enable
them, at least temporarily, to keep the problem from seriously jeopardizing family unity and the physical or emotional
health of individual members.

The degree to which they are able to cope and the level
at which they resolve their problems are crucial considerations
for treatment planning. Service would be geared to greater
depth than that proposed for the preceding group. In addition
to a resolution of crises and relief from immediate distress,
the social worker would attempt to educate the family regarding the pattern of behavior which gave rise to problems and to
effect some modification in these patterns through a variety of
approaches fitted to the client's situation. Techniques may include changing the role performance of family members, modifying their adaptive patterns, or allocating new roles wherever
the social structure permits it. In some instances the social
worker, through his broker role, will be able to modify role
norms.

Intervention at this second level of treatment, in contrast to the previous one, calls for more intensive services:
counselling for problems of behavior and interpersonal relations; more extensive effort at getting the family to make
fuller and better use of community resources; innovative services when a scarcity of resources makes it impossible to
meet family needs; help to change interactional patterns in

the family and also with the extended family, friends, neighbors, and employers. Where the social environment is particularly unfavorable and inflexible, intervention of this sort may require the family to make changes in living arrangements or employment.

The direct association found between family malfunctioning and socio-economic status has special implications for intervention in Near Problematic families. It means, in effect, that for these families there is a special need to explore the nexus between intrafamilial malfunctioning and unemployment, inadequate income, debts, financial worries, and poor housing. These may be the issues that need to be given priority, with emphasis on such tangible services as job training, job finding, day care services, supplementation of public assistance payment, and the procurement of better housing. Health problems did not figure prominently among the young families in the sample, but there may be individual cases where there is need for health services.

Intervention with problematic families. Intervention to improve the social functioning of Problematic families starts from the empirically based premise that this more extreme form of malfunctioning constitutes an interlocking of malfunctioning in many areas--Family Relationships, Individual Behavior, Care and Training of Children, Social Activities, plus the instrumental areas, particularly Economic and Household Conditions and Practices. Some of these families are truly multi-problem in the sense that their functioning represents a threat to the well-being of one or more family members. Others show behavior that is potentially dangerous to family welfare.

Problematic families, with few exceptions, are deprived families. Here, as in the Near Problematic group, the most appropriate strategy of service may be early assistance to improve the housing and economic situation. Help with these matters can open the door for intervention in areas of Individual Behavior and Family Relationships, as well as Care and Training of Children.

Intervention to cope with the more serious intra- and interpersonal problems requires intensive counselling and, in cases of serious pathology, referral for specialized treatment.

Widespread socio-economic deprivation in the Problematic group calls for an intervention program backed by resources to increase economic security and to raise the standard of living. Where earning potential is absent or limited, an income maintenance program must be made available. Beyond that, deprived and malfunctioning families need to experience a degree of achievement and success in family life, which the social worker can help them achieve by giving active guidance, perhaps even performing certain tasks presently beyond the competence of the family, at least until they are learned and incorporated through imitation. As in the Near Problematic families, intervention here must maximize efforts to help the families establish a connection with the larger social structure of the community so as to reduce isolation and bring about better use of resources.

Intervention with the Problematic as well as the Near Problematic group of families often means providing economic, social, and emotional props for the single or deserted mother, whether she lives alone or with parents or relatives. Her functioning was found to be significantly more problematic than that of the married mother in the same status group. Service to the unmarried or deserted mother, while utilizing some or all of the techniques used in working with those who have husbands, is likely to focus especially upon problems inherent in her relationship to the social network. For mothers living in social isolation the establishment of activity and educational peer groups may be indicated.

All in all, intervention in the lives of Problematic families, in contrast to treatment for Adequate and Near Adequate families, calls for a heavy reliance upon service in the instrumental areas. While the cause and effect relationship between malfunctioning in expressive and instrumental areas remains hypothetical, our program of intervention is guided by the assumption that there is greater vulnerability to overall problem functioning in the instrumentally handicapped families. The approach which advocates beginning treatment by helping the client with tangible problems that he himself has clearly identified has long been preferred by social workers serving the economically deprived population, and to this we subscribe.

Roles and functions of the intervenor. Whatever the social functioning level of the families he is aiding, the social worker must establish himself as a primary community resource and a channel of other existing resources. As intervenor he provides information, guidance, and advice by consulting with or bringing in professional specialists; he acts as mediator and communications link between client and resource, and whenever possible he functions directly as counselor, enabler, and problem-solver.

Bringing community resources or even knowledge of their existence to the family may serve to prevent crisis or breakdown in the future. When using community resources, early intervention is most likely to be truly preventive if the services are directed toward coping with possible, anticipated problematic functioning rather than the solution of existing problems. The worker will seek to enhance the client's communication skill when dealing with the community agencies and services likely to serve as a resource for different kinds of problems. Granted that such resources in the American community are scarce and generally underdeveloped, we nonetheless postulate that non-use by potential clients is to no small measure the result of an absence of knowledge about them and a lack of social skill on the part of those families who deal with them. If appropriate community facilities and services are indeed absent, the intervention agency should, whenever possible, act as an extra resource which, in one form or another, will find the means to render assistance to the family either by creating makeshift resources or stretching existing services to cover them.

The social worker engaged in preventive services who attempts to bring deficient or poorly developed resources to the family will find himself playing two somewhat non-traditional roles: those of the broker and the advocate.[14] As a broker he will serve as an intermediary between the client and the agency, seeking to bring about policy changes at the local level for groups of people such as those with which he is dealing. As an advocate he argues the client's point of view with an eye toward modifying agency policy and/or practice. In both roles the worker takes a partisan position, particularly when he acts the advocate who had, in fact, decided that the client is not receiving his due.

Let us now operationally recast much of the foregoing statement on intervention strategy and the role and function of the worker in a form which permits empirical exploration and an assessment of patterns of intervention.

Operationalizing Intervention

While the strategy of intervention sketched above provided important guidelines for the Project's supervisory staff

in designing treatment plans based on profiles of family functioning, it did not, nor was it intended to, address itself to
the actual activities of worker and client as they constitute
the woof and warp of the interventive process. Both from
research and clinical perspectives it became essential to explore the intervention process at a more microscopic level
in order to be able to relate outcome to service input and
thus be in a position to know which patterns of intervention
to replicate. Following a rather thoroughgoing review of the
literature on psychotherapy research and studies of social
interaction in general,[15] it was decided that the nature of
worker-client activity, which takes a variety of forms, could
be most meaningfully studied as a process of social exchange.

Intervention process as social exchange. The method
of analysis used to study the social exchange process was
based on Richard Longabaugh's system for coding interpersonal behavior.[16] The theoretical roots of Longabaugh's
schema are to be found in the writings of John W. Thibaut
and Harold H. Kelley and George Homans.[17]

Briefly stated, analysis of the process of social exchange utilized two dimensions: the resource exchanged or
"the things which the people value in one another and attempt
to secure from one another,"[18] and the modes of interaction
which Longabaugh defines as "modalities of exchange," comprising the acts of seeking, offering, depriving, accepting,
and not-accepting.[19] Resources exchanged are of three kinds:
information, direction (Longabaugh calls it control[20]) and support, and for obvious reasons, it will be referred to subsequently as the IDS exchange system of analysis.

This coding schema, which will be elaborated below,
was used in conjunction with a recording device referred to
earlier as the Treatment Log.[21]

Recording the intervention process. The Treatment
Log [reproduced in Appendix F] was designed to record in an
abbreviated form all of a social worker's activity involving
interviews, telephone conversations, and letters on behalf of
the client family. The Log was set up to enable the worker
to record one week's case activity for each member of a family seen. It covered the following items: identifying information, the date of the contact, the subjects discussed, the persons involved, the place and mode of contact, by whom the
contact was initiated, the worker's activity, and the activity
of the client or collateral.

The worker assigned to the case had sole responsibility for filling in the weekly Treatment Log, recording the weekly interaction between the client and him- or herself for a given category and sub-category of family functioning as defined by the St. Paul Scale of Family Functioning. This format enabled the researchers to relate the intervention process to changes in family functioning.

When recording both his own and the client's activity and attitude, the worker attempted to capture the "back and forth" interaction between the two of them by describing sequentially what each one did and said about any given topic. In addition, the worker recorded the feeling tone that accompanied a client's activity. Although the worker numbered his exchanges with the client to represent the sequence in which it took place, this does not mean that the entire interview as it occurred was replicated. As with most spontaneous conversations, a given topic might have been discussed at several different points in the course of the interview and the worker was instructed to record this discussion in the Log as though it had occurred continuously rather than intermittently. Admittedly, for those who would emphasize the overriding importance of subject contiguity in the client's defensive maneuvering, this was a distortion of the temporal integrity of the process. The objection, of course, rests on the choice of research perspectives. It registers preference for an analysis of the nature of individual interview sessions, while the process indicated here favors identifying the basic elements of exchange and analyzing their patterns over the total span of intervention rather than by more microscopic units of time.

In addition to the conceptual linking of the weekly Treatment Log and the St. Paul Scale of Family Functioning through their common organization around sub-categories of social functioning, there was substantive integration as well. In preparing profiles of family functioning at six month intervals during the period of intervention, treatment workers relied heavily upon the content of Logs, thus further promoting a common basis for relating process to outcome.

The information recorded by the worker on the Treatment Logs constituted the raw data which was coded by research workers using the IDS (Information-Direction-Support) exchange system of analysis. We are aware of the problems pertaining to the reliability and validity of material recorded by the caseworker who is personally involved in treating the client family, as compared to the recording of worker-client interaction by either a third party or completely mechanical means (video-sound equipment).[22] However, because of the size of the population served, a desire to observe the entire intervention process rather than sample it, and the sensitive nature of the treatment process itself, neither mechanical recording device nor third party observation was feasible. Therefore, the Treatment Log (structured in most portions and semi-structured in the remaining areas) was viewed as the optimal available recording system when it was accompanied by close research-oriented supervision. Furthermore, the nature of the data analysis (to be discussed below) which focused on a very large number of observations per case was seen as a further mitigant of bias. Certainly we cannot claim to have eliminated this persistent methodological problem which continues to harass process research in general.

    Coding intervention records. In the course of three years over 10,000 Treatment Logs were accumulated on the 272 families in the treatment group. The number of Logs per family ranged from two or three for families that dropped out of the study during its early weeks, to close to 100 Logs on families whose situation not only necessitated frequent worker-client contact but more than one Log sheet during certain weeks in order to record the involved nature of the intervention. With this very large number of Treatment Logs and roughly five times that number of units of analysis-- the reader will recall that each Log contained five subject discussed-activity units--it was obvious that the coding scheme would have to be amenable to electronic data processing.

    The coding procedure[23] involved the transfer of the information from a single weekly Treatment Log to a code sheet [see sample in Appendix G] and finally onto a data processing card. Each card was identified by case and its sequence within the case as determined by the week of treatment it represented. Thus, it was possible to determine not only the number of contacts between worker and client, but the spacing of contacts over the three-year period of intervention as well. Furthermore, the approximate amount of time spent per visit was recorded as well as the place and mode of contact. Counts and frequency distributions of these data provide some basic information on service input.

    The major portion of the Log and therefore each corresponding data card was devoted to information on worker-client activity. First the coders read the entire set of Logs

for one case and then re-read and coded each week of service. From pre-coded lists on the code sheet itself they
identified numbers for the subject discussed, the discussants,
and the initiators of the discussion for each week's five predominant topics. (As inferred above, more than five distinct
subjects could have been discussed in one week, in which
case coders were instructed to use more than one data card.)
Corresponding to each of the five columns covering the subject discussed were five sets of worker-client activity columns.
In each of these sets of columns, the coder specified the worker's activity in terms of whether the worker asked for, offered, gave, accepted or rejected information, direction, support, practical help, or analysis. In similar fashion the
client's activity around that particular subject was coded.

Several further comments regarding the coding procedure need to be made, involving the notion of worker-client
activity versus worker-client interaction, modifications made
on Longabaugh's category system of exchange analysis, and
the reliability of our coding method in general.

During the early development of the IDS coding system,
the term activity, or action, was substituted for the term interaction so as to avoid restricting the coding to only those
situations in which a clear action-reaction interactive unit was
observed. Units of worker or client activity recorded by workers were coded even when their response or elicited reactions
had not been recorded and therefore could not be coded. The
nature of the abbreviated recording by workers simply did not
permit the reconstruction of complex interactive units; hence,
the term activity analysis, rather than interaction analysis,
was adopted. This shift in perspective did not have a major
impact upon data analysis.

To Longabaugh's three basic categories of resources
exchanged--information, direction and support--the FLIP coding system added practical help and analysis. These addi-
tions were required to provide categories for the helping be-
haviors not considered in the Longabaugh system which had
been designed to tap interaction between mother-child dyads.
Our five category resource typology comprised 1) information--
defined as a verbal communication that seeks or provides
knowledge about relevant situations, persons, feelings, or
attitudes, not aimed at effecting a change in the other's behavior, attitudes, or feelings; 2) direction--verbal communication attempting to control, guide, or decrease the number
of possible courses of action available to the other person;

3) support--verbal or non-verbal (though recorded, of course) communication which attempts to emotionally sustain the other person (s) through expression of approval, encouragement, or comfort;   4) practical help--verbal or non-verbal communication that offers or provides any concrete service such as transportation, money, goods, language translation, escort, etc.; and   5) analysis--a series of verbal communications which attempt to show relationships between actions or attitudes and their motives with one or more of the following objectives: a) identifying and explaining the client's feelings and behavior, b) explaining why others behave in a certain way toward the client, c) reviewing with the client what has happened thus far in the course of intervention, and d) explaining or interpreting nonverbal action of the client's.

The final list of modes of exchange employed by the FLIP or IDS system is as follows: asking for, offering, giving, accepting, and rejecting. These modes of exchange differed insignificantly from Longabaugh's earlier noted list of modes.[24] One further addition to the IDS system permitted the coding of the worker's observation on the client's positive or negative effect.

The attainment of high degrees of inter-coder reliability was a priority, both in the initial training of coders and later during the continuous monitoring which was maintained throughout the coding operation. During their closely supervised and intensive training, coders were paired for practice coding in all possible combinations and these were continued until the team attained an inter-coder reliability of 80% or better. Beyond that point each coder worked alone. However, on approximately every sixth case taken randomly, quality control checks of inter-coder reliability were obtained, controlled for pairings of coders to assure balance. In this manner 33 quality control measures yielded the following inter-coder reliability figures on areas of Treatment Log coding susceptible to judgement error by coders:

Area of Coding Tested	Mean Percentage of Agreement	Standard Deviation
Subject Discussed	89%	6%
Initiator of Discussion	91%	6%
Worker Activity	87%	7%
Client Activity	91%	5%

Analysis of coded data. In analyzing the data accumulated through the methods described above, the objective was to seek out those patterns of psychological and social resources exchanged between worker and client over the course of intervention that appear to have enhanced family functioning or, at least, to have retarded dysfunction. There are four principal points of reference in the following analysis: 1) The temporal patterning of intervention, which can be viewed as a structural characteristic; 2) the process of resource exchange including the persons involved and content of the exchange; 3) the type and relative mix of resources exchanged, or the substantive aspect of intervention; 4) the relationship of the preceding factors to intervention outcome.

In exploring patterns of intervention, a two-step approach has been employed. Initially, data is presented in an inventory fashion so that an overall picture can be obtained; then patterns of data are explored. Thus, in reference to temporal structuring, for example, inventory data on the total number of visits and the average number of visits per six-month treatment period are presented, followed by indices of visiting patterns over time as related to selected dependent variables.

Central to the exploration of intervention is the role of the worker, and aspects of this particular variable will be viewed from both "cause" and "effect" perspectives; that is, factors appearing to determine worker style and its effect upon outcome will be explored.

Throughout the analysis, statistical measures of association and significance will be used in assessing the relationship among variables; however, where the number of cases is too small to permit the use of statistical tests of significance, percentage comparisons alone must suffice.

Intervention Patterns and
Change in Family Functioning

There are two perspectives from which we will examine patterns of intervention and their relationship to change in family functioning. First we will focus on the components of the treatment program and their effect on family functioning for the client group as a whole, after which we will seek to identify characteristic patterns of worker intervention, differentiating the effective workers from their less successful colleagues.

The temporal pattern of intervention. For the purposes of the analysis at hand, the intervention phase of the
Family Life Improvement Project which lasted three years
has been divided into six 6-month treatment periods. The
modal length of participation was five treatment periods with
68 families (39% of the population served) receiving services
of 30 months' duration. Thirty-four families (19%) were in
treatment from the beginning to the end of the Project; 50
families (28%) participated during four treatment periods;
and the remainder, 25 families (14%), received services for
three periods (18 months) or less. There are a number of
reasons why families received fewer than six treatment periods. At the outset there was a need for FLIP workers to
work primarily with those families which presented relatively
more problematic profiles of family functioning; there was
difficulty in locating families that had moved between the
time of first contact with the Project and the beginning of
treatment; and at two points during the duration of the Project there was worker turn-over.

The number of visits per family ranged widely, depending mainly upon the need for service. At the lower end
of the distribution were 13 families (7% of the population
served) with nine visits or less; at the upper end were nine
families (5%) who were visited 63 times or more. Between
these extremes, 48 families (27%) had a total of 12 visits,
the modal visiting frequency. The distribution of visit frequency for the entire period is shown below:

No. of Visits	No. of Families	% of Pop. Served
Fewer than 9	13	7%
9 - 11	24	14%
12	34	19%
13 - 24	48	27%
25 - 48	36	21%
49 - 62	13	7%
63 or more	9	5%
	177	100%

The mean number of visits per six-month treatment
period also varied considerably. There were four families
who were seen only once per period and two families who
were visited on the average of 16 times or more. The following, however, is the more typical pattern. Two visits:

47 families (27%); three to four visits: 61 families (or 35% of the population served); five to six visits: 20 families (11%); and seven to eight visits: 18 families (10%). The remaining 25 families (14%) had between nine and 15 visits per treatment period.

Mean No. of Visits per Treatment Period	No. of Families	% of Pop. Served
1	4	2%
2	47	27%
3 - 4	61	35%
5 - 6	20	11%
7 - 8	18	10%
9 - 15	25	14%
16 or more	2	1%
	177	100%

Both total number of treatment visits and the average number of visits per treatment period are associated with beginning St. Paul Family Functioning Scores and the presence of problems[25] in social functioning. Lower beginning scores and problemicity are found to be correlated with more frequent visits. (Total number of visits and beginning family functioning score: $C = .47,$[26] $x^2 = 50.51$, 6 d.f., $p < .001$; average number of visits and beginning family functioning score: $C = .46$, $x^2 = 48.56$, 4 d.f., $p < .001$; total number of visits and problemicity: $C = .41$, $x^2 = 35.26$, 6 d.f., $p < .001$; average number of visits and problemicity: $C = .41$, $x^2 = 35.15$, 6 d.f., $p < .001$.) This finding, of course, is completely in keeping with the strategy of intervention as it calls for the frequency and intensity of service to be related to need, determined by the level of social functioning.

In an effort to explore changes in the frequency of visits over the course of intervention, an index was developed indicating whether the number of visits to Project families had increased, decreased, or remained the same from treatment period to treatment period. Though a number of patterns emerged, we will focus on the overall trend. The predominant pattern for 41% of the population served (73 families), was a decrease in the number of visits as time elapsed. The next most frequently occurring pattern was that of a relatively constant number of visits from treatment period to treatment period, and it was observed in 32% of the cases (57 families). Finally, 27% of the population served (47 families) showed an increase in visit frequency over time.

Again, in keeping with treatment strategy, an association was found between low beginning family functioning score and problemicity and a visiting pattern of decreasing frequency (C's of .34 and .33, respectively, X^2's of 23.70 and 21.04, 6 and 9 d.f.'s, and significant beyond the .001 and .02 levels). This pattern results from the initial concentration of visits focused on early intervention with a subsequent diminution in the frequency of meetings. More adequately functioning families were maintained on either an evenly paced visiting pattern or one that increased as time elapsed and family needs grew.

When visiting pattern is cross-tabulated against movement, a positive statistically significant though weak association is found between the constant visiting patterns and improved family functioning scores (C = .25, X^2 = 12.23, 4 d.f., p < .02) but no significant association can be established between movement and total and average number of visits.

Table 13

The Relationship of Intervention Visiting Patterns and Change in Family Functioning Scores Among the Population Served

| | Intervention Visiting Patterns | | |
| | Visiting over time: | | |
Change in Family Functioning Scores	Increases (N=47)	Remains Constant (N=57)	Decreases (N=73)
Positive Change*	43%	68%	45%
No Change	23%	11%	16%
Negative Change	34%	21%	39%
	100%	100%	100%

C = .25, X^2 = 12.23, 4 d.f. p < .02

---

*N's for change score differ slightly from those presented in Chapter 6 where outcome was measured from the first Profile, while here it is based on the first treatment Profile.

Thus, though the total and average number of worker-client visits in and of themselves are not associated with movement, their patterning, that is, the changes in relative frequency during the treatment period which is a gross structural expression of service input, is related to movement. However, at this point it would not seem wise to search further among these variables for meaning. Certainly, until visiting patterns are related to substantive treatment inputs, no clear meaning can be extracted from these trends.

The process of resource exchange between worker and client. Thus far in exploring patterns of intervention, only passing mention has been made of the actors involved. As noted much earlier under methodological issues, a completely valid consideration of the intervention process is attainable only when thorough, precise, and objective recording procedures, preferably electronic, have been employed. Budget limitations prevented the use of such procedures on the originally substantial sample of 272 treatment families. The semistructured weekly Treatment Log, conceptually integrated with the St. Paul Scale of Family Functioning, was the most feasible procedure given the constraints of the reality at hand.

Some basic facts about the services. Central to the intervention strategy was a family centered focus in which all relevant family members were to be involved in treatment. The Project's goal of preventing emerging family disorganization also called for a reaching out strategy that placed heavy emphasis on early worker initiative in engaging the family in service. The extensiveness of these reaching out efforts can be roughly gauged by such indicators as the proportion of workers' time spent in direct service compared with other kinds of activities, and the mode and place of treatment. An estimate of the degree to which the treatment was family centered can be gained by identifying the participants in the treatment process. Finally, the effectiveness of the workers' efforts to engage clients in treatment can be inferred from the extent to which clients keep or fail to keep appointments.

FLIP workers indicated on their Treatment Logs that 73% of the time invested with the 177 families in the population served was spent in direct service activity. (Twenty-three percent of the remaining time expended on these families was involved in administrative duties, including recording, and four percent in supervision and training.) Eighty-two percent of the direct service work was rendered in person, 18% by phone. Approximately 89% of the worker's face-to-face contact with others was in the client's home, 11% at other community agency offices, and less than one percent on FLIP premises.

The client family, alone or in combination with another, was engaged by the worker in 83% of the service-rendering contacts. Within that category of contacts, 62% of the worker's time was spent with the young mother, 4% with her husband, and 3% with both her and her husband. The worker spent 4% of his or her time with the young mother and a relative and 8% of the time with a relative, other than the husband, alone. Two percent of worker time was spent in other contacts in which the client was a partner. Non-family service contacts, taking up 17% of worker time, involved other community agency personnel (in 1% of these the client accompanied the worker). These service program characteristics, then, can be summarized in the pattern flow as follows:

% of Service Time Spent in:		Participants		
Direct Service	73%	Client Family		83%
Administrative Duties	23%	Client Alone	62%	
Training & Supervision	4%	Relative Alone	8%	
	100%	Husband Alone	4%	
Place of Service			74%	
Client's Home	89%	Client & Relative	4%	
Community Agencies	11%	Client & Husband	3%	
FLIP Office (Less than)	1%		81%	
	100%			
Mode of Service		Client & Another		
Face-to-face	82%	Worker	1%	
Telephone	18%	Client & Other	1%	
	100%		83%	
		Other Worker Alone	17%	
			100%	

Generally speaking, treatment families made themselves readily available to their FLIP workers. It was the standard procedure for workers to arrange the time and date of visits with the client family beforehand; unannounced drop-in visits were rarely employed. An index expressing the number of completed interviews with a client family as a percentage of the total attempted contacts indicated that approximately 60%

of the population served kept 70% or more of their appointments.   Only 29 or 16% of the 177 families served required
a greater than two-to-one effort of attempts to successful
visits.   Considering the fact that completely voluntary participation by a randomly selected sample of young urban families meant contact with FLIP for from three-and-a-half to
four years, these figures on client accessibility are indeed
impressive.

Having considered these general program features, we
turn now to the process variables.   The unit of measure used
in examining the variation over time among the process variables is the treatment phase, which differs from the treatment period referred to previously.   A treatment phase consists of one third of the total number of contacts between
worker and client.   Since this number varied from family to
family, the frequency of contact within treatment phases also
varies from family to family.   It has been reasoned that
within the overall Project framework in which level of social
functioning along with treatment strategy determines the individual family's treatment plan, a unit of time specific to
the particular case is more effective in permitting measurement of variation in service input than would be an absolute
time unit such as the treatment period scheme used earlier.
The treatment period was a function of the Project's life span
rather than an indicant of the client's position in his course
of service.   When, for example, the second treatment phase
is discussed below, it shall thus be understood to represent
the middle third of the course of treatment for all families,
regardless of how long they were in treatment or how frequently they were visited.   Had the treatment period scheme
been employed similarly, a range of time midway into the
Project would not have caught all families at a comparable
point in their treatment, some of them actually being in the
middle of treatment, others just getting under way.

Discussants.   In examining the percentages which mark
the extent to which the nuclear unit, or young mother and father, were the discussants with the FLIP worker, fluctuation
moves from 84% for the first treatment phase to 86% for the
second and 88% for the third phase.   Other discussants shar-
ing the balance of these percentages were other community
agency workers and relatives;   the degree of their participation in discussion varied only slightly in the course of the
three treatment phases. [27]

Initiation of discussion.   Greater variation was found
in the extent to which the client initiated a subject of discus-

sion. For the three treatment phases considered together, the worker initiated 57% of the subjects, the client 37%. The remaining 6% again represents initiations by other workers and relatives. In line with the professional expectation that continued service permits a shifting of initiating from worker to client, it was found that the percentage of client-introduced discussions rose from 32% to 39% to 41% for phases I, II, and III, respectively. Correspondingly, the proportion for worker initiation fell from 62% to 55% to 54%. These are not spectacular changes, but they go in the direction suggested by widely accepted casework theory which views growth in direct initiative as evidence of growth in autonomy and self-assurance.

A more microscopic investigation into change patterns in initiation can be made by looking at shifts in the relative domination by the worker or client over treatment phases. Relative domination of discussion refers to the degree to which the initiation of discussion by the worker or the client increases or decreases relative to the initiations by the other.

As might be gathered from the foregoing figures on initiation patterns, the worker dominates in over half, 100 or 57% of the cases, but his dominance varies from phase to phase. Most typically, in 25% of the cases, worker domination rose from phase one to two, then fell in phase three to a point lower than the phase one level. In 15%, worker domination rises and falls but ends at a level higher than the beginning phase. In 5% of the cases, the worker dominates increasingly over each successive period.

In 56, or 31% of the cases, worker and client initiated discussions about equally. In 13% of the latter the worker dominated in phase one and two, the client dominated in phase three. In 11% the worker dominated in phase one and three, but the client was ascendant in phase two. Seven percent of the cases showed other miscellaneous patterns of shared worker-client domination.

Finally, in 21 or 12% of the cases, the client had the upper hand in initiating discussions. In 7% of these, client domination decreased from phase one to three and in 5%, client domination increased successively.

The subjects of discussion. The subjects of discussion between FLIP worker and client, originally coded by sub-areas of family functioning (after the St. Paul Scale),

were re-grouped for analysis into three categories corresponding to the problem typology presented at the outset of
the chapter.   These included: 1) expressive topics, 2) instrumental topics, and 3) role topics. Expressive topics refer to areas of functioning covered by the St. Paul categories
of Family Relationships and Unity, Social Activities, Relationship to the Worker, and the sub-area of training methods
and emotional care of the area Care and Training of Children.
Instrumental topics comprise St. Paul areas of functioning
entitled Economic Practices, Health Conditions and Practices,
Home and Household Practices, Use of Community Resources,
and the sub-area physical care under Care and Training of
Children.   Role topics refer to the Individual Behavior and
Adjustment of every family member. [28]

     Discussion with FLIP families was heavily oriented
toward instrumental functioning (46% of the subjects covered),
denoting in effect that the eight Project social workers addressed themselves to such immediate practical problems as
employment, health, housing, and running the home.   Expressive functioning constituted the content of a third (33%)
of the subjects discussed, while role behavior occupied a
fifth (20%) of the discussion material. [29]

     Changes in content from treatment phases one to three
were small but consistent, showing slight increases in the
content of expressive functioning (33%, 34%, 34%) and role
functioning 19%, 20%, 22%) at the expense of instrumental
functioning (48%, 46%, 44%).   Once again, this change is in
line with expectations regarding professional casework practice, according to which a continued worker-client relationship will tend to focus increasingly on individual and interpersonal behavior.

     Shifts in salient content from the first to the last
treatment phases represent a variety of the possible patterns
of combinations and permutations.   Only the four most prevalent patterns involving the great majority of the cases
(159 or 90%) are reported.   For these 159 families, discussion remained on instrumental topics in 59% of the cases,
shifted from instrumental to expressive in 18% of the cases,
remained on expressive topics in 14% of the cases, and shifted from expressive to instrumental topics in the remaining
9%.

     Whether a family shifted in the predominant subject
matter discussed over time was associated with its beginning

family functioning score (C = .29, X^2 = 15.84, 8 d.f., p <
.05). Most of the families that shifted from expressive to
instrumental topics were in the high range of family functioning (53% as contrasted with 27% in the mid-range of scores
and 20% in the low range). This is consistent with practice
strategy since early contacts with more adequately functioning families would not be focused on job, health, etc. Also,
in keeping with expectations is the observation that 52% of the
high-beginning-score families maintained predominantly expressive discussion throughout the Project (as contrasted to
39% of the mid-range scorers and 9% of the low-range scorers), and correspondingly, 45% of the low-beginning-score
families (as contrasted to 26 and 29% of the high-and-medium-
range scorers) focused on instrumental topics throughout their
tenure. Among the 62 families with low beginning scores,
42 or 68% remained instrumentally oriented in discussion.
Only two low scoring families began and ended with predominantly expressive discussion, while 13% or eight families
shifted from instrumental to expressive topics.

When type of presenting problem is cross-tabulated
against changes in expressive discussion, it is noted that the
greatest decrease over time is among clients who presented
expressive problems at the outset. A similar decrease in
instrumental discussion with families presenting instrumental
problems also occurs. Departing from this trend, however,
role discussion continuously increases over time, regardless
of the type or even the presence of problem.

Among none of the problem types is increased worker
dominance in initiation of subject matter found to be a typical pattern. In all problem types, save instrumental, the
modal pattern was a relative decrease in worker dominance
in the initiation of matters to be discussed. With instrumental problems, the modal pattern was represented by the client
attaining dominance in the second treatment phase, followed
by the worker returning to dominance in the third phase. This
middle phase of peaked client activity can be viewed as the
point at which the client is most actively involved in following
through upon an agreed plan of seeking out community resources to aid instrumental functioning, while frequently reporting back to the Project worker with developments. Similar activity is not characteristic of clients with expressive
problems where a continuous psychological counselling process is more stabilized in its gradual weaning of client from
the worker.

It is interesting to note that in the 21 cases where the client was dominant over the entire course of intervention, 15 presented no problematic functioning, three had expressive problems, two instrumental problems, and only one family had a combination of instrumental-expressive and role problems.

In drawing together this material relating to discussants, subjects discussed, and initiation-dominance of discussion, we found that the trends in process patterns over time adhered to the intervention strategy--in which reaching out, family-centered workers would take early action with the instrumentally malfunctioning, then move on to concern with expressive and role problems. However, we failed to find that these activity patterns in and of themselves were associated with change in family functioning scores. Of course, as when temporal patterns were examined alone, activity patterns, which are devoid of substantive content, can convey little of the work of change. We shall turn next, therefore, to the substantive issue of the type and the mix of resources exchanged.

The type and mix of resources exchanged. The FLIP client had two sources of service input, his Project worker and, in addition, any other community agency workers with whom his family was involved. The latter group could include health, education, welfare, housing, employment, and legal agency workers. If a family was receiving services from a community agency, then from the Project's perspective, the FLIP worker's roles might variously be those of coordinator, monitor, advocate, or consultant. Thus, the potential list of resources to be exchanged between worker and client went beyond those of information, direction, support, practical help, and analysis; it included activities of service coordination and/or intercession by the worker on behalf of his client with community agencies.

By far the most frequently exchanged resource was information, and its predominant flow was from client to worker. Over 80% of the client's activity during treatment interviews was composed of providing the worker with information.[30] Correspondingly, 60% of the worker's activity was devoted to asking the client for information. The reverse flow of information, from worker to client, comprised roughly 18% of the worker's activity and requests for such information on the client's part constituted a similar 18% of his activity in treatment.

The next most frequently exchanged resource was support provided to the client by the worker. This activity made up 10% of the worker's overall effort. The provision of direction or advice and guidance comprised a further 6% of the worker's activity; practical help, and service coordination and intercession on the client's behalf constituted 5% of his effort. The remaining 1% of worker activity was devoted to analysis, as defined earlier in the chapter.[31]

None of the resources exchanged varied appreciably over time. When the total number of visits was divided into three equivalent treatment phases, the amount of information exchanged varied 5 to 6% over the course of intervention, while the other resources varied by a percentage point or two.

Though this general inventory of resources exchanged indicated that information predominated over all other resources by a substantial three to one margin when total number of worker-client exchanges formed the basis of comparison, two points of qualification demand emphasis. First, the base figure involved, the total number of worker-client exchanges, was of such a magnitude $(70,000)$[32] that a 1 or 2% incidence of resource utilization still represented a substantial number. Additionally, since information exchange as a preliminary and exploratory activity is fundamental to the interview process, we regarded a single exchange of practical help, direction, support, or analysis as being of relatively greater significance than a single exchange of information. The data indicated that although exchanges of direction, support, analysis, and practical help occurred with only one-quarter the frequency of informational exchanges, 93% of the population served, all but 12 families, received some support. Similarly, 84% of all families served received some direction, 63% some practical help, and 54% some analysis.

Just how much of a resource or service input a family received was related, in general, to its beginning family functioning score and the presence of problematic functioning--again as would be expected in accordance with the intervention strategy. The amount of direction supplied by workers was significantly associated with low beginning family functioning scores $(X^2 = 17.72, 6 \text{ d.f.}, p < .01, C = .31)$ and with problemicity $(X^2 = 17.24, 9 \text{ d.f.}, p < .05, C = .30)$. The amount of practical help was associated with low beginning family functioning scores $(X^2 = 60.44, 6 \text{ d.f.}, p < .001,$

C = .50) and with problemicity (X^2 = 45.90, 9 d.f., p < .001, C = .45). And, the amount of service coordination and intercession by FLIP workers with other community agency workers was also significantly associated with low beginning family functioning scores and problemicity (X^2 = 21.83, 2 d.f., p < .001, C = .33 for the former and X^2 = 21.15, 3 d.f., p < .001, C = .33 for the latter).

It is noteworthy that neither the amount of information exchanged nor support supplied were significantly associated with either low scores for beginning family functioning or problemicity. The first of these two findings is not particularly surprising in light of the argument cited above, that information exchange is a rather generic resource basic to the interviewing technique of exploration--and here it might be added that it was necessary with adequate as well as less adequate families in this research-action study.

However, our second finding, that there was no significant association between the amount of support supplied and family functioning scores or problemicity, was not anticipated. Percentage analysis of cross-tabulations of these three variables indicates that more support was given by workers to higher scoring and non-problematic families than to less adequately functioning families. Support, it will be recalled, could take the form of approval, encouragement, or comfort, and though it might be suggested that support primarily in the form of praise and approval was about the only resource other than information workers saw as appropriate for adequately functioning families, it is unclear why they used even less support in the form of encouragement with families in difficulty. Focus on more instrumentally oriented and directive techniques with this problematic group might provide one explanation; however, no data can be offered in support of such an hypothesis.

Before moving on to comment on the association of resources exchanged with change in family functioning scores, we might note here, somewhat parenthetically, that among 85% of the population served there was some exchange of information and direction pertaining to the use of community resources or the services of other community health, welfare, housing, employment, or legal agencies. Thirty-eight percent of these discussions dealt with welfare agencies--either county, city, or state child welfare agencies. Next in frequency were employment services, affecting 21% of the discussions. Employment services, as the term is used here, includes em-

ployment counseling, job training, and job finding and placement. The third most frequently discussed community resource, with 14% of the families, was that related to health
institutions and services. Remaining client concern centered
on legal services and law enforcement agencies in 7% of the
cases, public housing and Planned Parenthood services in 6%
of the cases each. The residual group of 8% was concerned
with a wide range of agency services not in the above set of
categories, among which there was a one percent concern for
day care services for the very young. Though associated with
problemicity as would be fully expected (x^2 = 26.98, 2 d.f.,
p < .001, C = .36), discussion of community resources bore
no significant relationship to change in family functioning
scores.

Returning to consider the relationship between resource
exchange and change in family functioning scores, we note in
Table 14 that the amount of direction and analysis given by
worker, and the amount of FLIP coordination and intercession
with other community agency workers are all significantly associated but in an unanticipated direction with change in family
functioning. The unexpected aspect of these findings is that
though the associations are weak they are in a negative direction.

Table 14

The Association of Resources Exchanged with Change in
Family Functioning Scores Among the Population Served

Resources Exchanged	Significance and Degree of Association with Change in Family Functioning Scores				
	x^2	d.f.	Sig.	C	Gamma
Direction	17.25	6	p < .01	.30	-.11
Analysis	8.71	2	p < .02	.22	-.21
Coordination	7.30	2	p < .05	.20	-.25

Examination of the data on which these statistics are
based shows that 72% of the 29 families receiving no direction
from their workers improved their scores as compared to 48%
improving in family functioning scores among those receiving
direction, while only 10% of the families who did not receive
direction declined in level of functioning, 35% of the families
who received it, did. Similarly, though less dramatically,

the functioning of 44% of the 82 families who received analysis declined while only 23% of those who did not receive analysis also declined. Finally, one half of the families receiving coordinated services showed negative movement at the end of intervention while only 28% of those not receiving coordinated services declined. The same trend although not at a level of statistical significance holds for the amount of support provided by workers. Nine families, or 75% of the 12 families not receiving support, improved in functioning while 50% of those families to whom we provided support declined in their level of social functioning.

The one instance of a statistically significant, positive association between a resource exchanged and change in family functioning was the amount of analysis given by the client (X^2 = 12.32, 2 d.f., p < .01, C = .26). This association is consistent with theory which holds that the client's engagement in an examination of his and others feelings, attitudes, and behavior is a growth promoting activity. It is surprising, however, to find this rather subtle and comparatively more sophisticated resource attaining statistically significant association with movement where others did not. This is perhaps not wholly unrelated to the fact that analysis is one of only two resources that could be exchanged in both directions-- from client to worker as well as from worker to client. The other resource, information, has already been discussed as a more generic commodity, too broadly employed to achieve specifically critical significance.

Related to the above, it should be mentioned that the readings taken on the client's affective orientation toward his worker were not associated with change in family functioning scores over the course of intervention, or with any other variable tested, for that matter. This is not a particularly unexpected finding since, more than any other variable studied, the worker's recording of client affect was most subject to selective recall and reporting. Somewhat consoling in reference to suspicions of recording bias, therefore, was the absence of a run-away trend in the reporting of positive affect.

In summary, then, the following four points can be made in reference to the type and mix of resources exchanged by worker and client: First, in terms of the absolute number of exchanges, information was by far the most frequently exchanged resource accounting for the vast bulk of the workers' and clients' activity. Nevertheless, it was also observed that other resources, though comprising only between a quarter and a fifth of worker-client activity, were exchanged in a large majority of cases: 93% of the population served received some support, 84% some direction, 63% some practical help (the figure in this instance includes coordination and intercession of services with other community agencies), and 54% of the families received some analysis.

Second, the relative amount of direction and practical help exchanged was seen to be significantly related to low beginning family functioning scores and degree of problemicity. By contrast, a non-significant relationship was noted for amount of support exchanged, suggesting that this resource was used as a reward for adequately functioning families with greater frequency than as an encouragement to the less adequately functioning family. The lack of a relationship between the amount of information exchanged and beginning family functioning scores and problemicity led to the interpretation that basic interviewing technique required its employment in exploration both toward treatment and research ends with the adequate as well as the less adequately functioning.

Third, the significant association discovered between the amount of analysis given by the client and change in family functioning scores suggested that the client's ability to engage in self-examination contributed to the family's improved social functioning.

Fourth, and yet to be comprehended, was the finding of significant though negative associations between the amount of direction, analysis, and worker coordination exchanged and improved family functioning over the course of intervention. An attempt to understand this finding will be made below as attention is turned to the role of the worker, patterns of intervention, and change in family functioning.

The worker, patterns of intervention, and change in family functioning. In order to provide a useful basis for readily distinguishing among the eight FLIP workers, we shall begin by ranking them in terms of the degree of movement or change in family functioning scores over the course of intervention within their respective caseloads, and from then on refer to each of them by their rank order. The data are shown in Table 15.

As can be observed in Table 15 five of the eight caseworkers are within six percentage points of one another in the amount of positive movement or change in family functioning

Table 15

Change in Family Functioning Scores and Other Factors Used to Rank Worker Caseloads in Terms of Intervention Outcome

Worker	Size of Caseload	Direction of Change in Family Function Scores			Cases with Problematic Functioning	Cases Headed by Un-wed Mothers	Weighted Score*
		Positive	None	Negative			
1	24	88%	8%	4%	50%	54%	284
2	19	63%	11%	26%	55%	47%	237
3	29	52%	31%	17%	17%	21%	235
4	19	48%	26%	26%	35%	42%	222
5	14	50%	14%	36%	64%	43%	214
6	24	50%	8%	42%	46%	33%	208
7	24	46%	8%	46%	42%	33%	200
8	24	13%	20%	67%	44%	21%	146

*By assigning a factor of 3 to positive change, 2 to no change, and 1 to negative change and multiplying each factor by the percentage of cases within the category and summing these, we obtained a weighted score.

within their caseloads. Workers 3 through 7 ranged from a
high of 52% to a low of 46% in the amount of improvement
within their caseloads. Worker 1 had an 88% rate of improvement and Worker 2 a 63% rate, while Worker 8, at the
other end of the distribution, had a 13% rate representing
the improvement of only three of her 24 families.

It can readily be observed that caseloads differed in
size from 29 to 14 families. At the outset of the Project,
the original treatment group of 272 families was randomly
and evenly divided into eight caseloads. However, families
were subsequently shifted from one caseload to another, rather thoroughly undoing the original random assignment. These
shifts were necessitated to insure language compatability a-
mong the Spanish-speaking and to adjust for the effects of
sample attrition and worker turnover.

Worker 3 with 29 families had the Project's largest
caseload at the end of intervention. Worker 5, with the Project's smallest caseload of 14 families at the end of treatment, was the only part-time caseworker. The two caseloads
with 19 families each, assigned to Workers 2 and 4, had experienced worker turnover. The remaining four caseloads
all had 24 families in treatment at the end of intervention.

Though with numerous departures from the original
random assignment, caseloads did vary from one another in
respect to their proportional shares of population characteristics, but in no instance were these variations found to be
statistically significant. Similarly, none of the intervention vari-
ables--which include temporal patterns of intervention, process
variables, and resource variables--could be shown to be significantly correlated with outcome by caseload. There were, however, a number of trends in the data that merit reporting.

With regard to the demographic characteristics of the
population served, race and social class were totally unpro-
ductive in discriminating outcome among caseloads. This was
not the case with marital status, however. A Spearman r
of +.604 (falling short of the statistically significant r_s of
+.643 for an N of 8 at the .05 level), indicated a tendency
toward correlation between the proportion of unwed mothers
in a worker's caseload and that worker's outcome ranking.
No easy explanation is available for this relationship because
marital status per se was not related to favorable outcome,
although lower beginning functioning which does correlate
strongly with positive movement was also associated directly

with out-of-wedlock motherhood.   The positive relationship
between percent of unmarried clients in caseload and proportion of successful outcomes may reflect an interaction effect
among these two and perhaps other factors (workers reported
for instance greater accessibility on the part of unmarried
mothers although this variable was not studied systematically)
which by themselves are not significantly related to treatment
outcome.

Examination of data trends related to the type and mix
of resources exchanged suggests that those workers who not
only gave greater amounts of support (r_S = +.619) but increased the amount of support given over the course of treatment (r_S = +.601) were the more successful workers.   Relatively more successful workers were also characterized by
their intercession on behalf of the client with other community
agencies (r_S = +.601), by their tendency to give increasing
amounts of information to the client (r_S = +.597), and by
their clients' tendencies to engage in analyzing their own behavior and situations (r_S = +.572).

A profile of resource exchange resulting in a relatively
more successful outcome does begin to emerge from these
data.   The picture of the more successful worker giving information, support, and coordinated service, with his client
participating in analysis contrasts with the relatively less
successful pattern of worker initiated analysis, direction,
practical help, and information seeking, as will be shown below.   The successful worker, it would thus appear, took a
less controlling role in intervention, using inputs of information and support rather than direction, analysis, or practical
help in his efforts to aid clients.   His use of support would
also suggest a more encompassing concern for the affective
dimension of the helping process.   Clients of successful workers seemed to have been more actively involved in treatment.
They engaged in an analysis of their own behavior and situations while the clients of less successful workers passively,
received insights from their workers.   The clients of successful workers, receiving fewer inputs of direction and practical help, made use of the information and coordinated services provided to emerge as more adequately functioning individuals at the end of treatment.   Generally speaking, then,
successful workers were less controlling, more supportive,
and elicited greater client engagement in treatment than their
less successful colleagues.

It is particularly interesting to note that the resource
exchange profile of the more successful workers does not

depart substantially from the overall patterning of resource exchange reported in the preceding section. In that section devoted to an examination of the type and mix of resources exchanged at the aggregate level, it will be recalled there resulted four statistically significant associations between particular resources and change in family functioning scores. The first three associations indicated a negative relationship between the workers' giving direction, analysis, and coordination of services and improved family functioning; the fourth association positively related a client's active participation in analyzing his situation with improved functioning. The roles of all four of these variables can be traced in our subsequent examination of the factors related to worker effectiveness rankings. We have already cited the data trend in the direction of a positive correlation between a client's participation in analysis and worker effectiveness (r_S = +.572, where an r_S = +.643 is significant at the .05 level). Not cited were the negative, though far from significant, correlations suggested by r_S's of -.333 and -.111 found between the amounts of direction and worker-initiated analysis exchanged respectively and the worker's effectiveness ranking. Thus, in three of the four instances the characteristic resource exchange profile of successful workers, though based only on less than statistically significant data trends, is substantially consistent with earlier significant findings on the type and mix of resource exchanged at the aggregate level.

More apparently contradictory, however, was the finding related to service coordination between FLIP and other community agency workers. The earlier resource exchange analysis indicated that worker intercession and coordination was negatively associated with movement. The subsequent worker effectiveness analysis indicated a tendency for intercession and coordination to become a positively correlated characteristic of the relatively more successful workers. These two findings need not be seen as contradictory, however, since both conditions could quite conceivably obtain simultaneously. That is to say, the more effective workers could have made relatively less frequent though more skillful use of community services on behalf of their clients, while at the same time a significant majority of all families receiving coordinated services could have failed to have benefited from them. There is every reason to believe that workers did indeed have to be quite skillful in dealing with the service structure within the city under study in order to assure benefit to their clients. Reading of the Treatment Logs indicated that particularly crucial on the worker's part was how he interpreted inadequate community services to the client. It has been suggested elsewhere in comparing the experiences of treatment and control group families with community services that a relatively more intensive exposure to negative experiences with other agencies may be one of the reasons treatment families scored lower in the Use of Community Resources than their control group counterparts.

The use of support by successful workers is of special interest at this juncture for it points once again both to the central and crucial role of individual worker skill at resource exchange and at the same time to the methodological limitations preventing a definitive evaluation of the processes involved. There was a great deal of support given by workers throughout the course of intervention. It was the second most frequently exchanged resource after information, and it was received in some amount by all but twelve families. So widespread was its employment that along with information no significant association could be uncovered between its use and client characteristics. There was some evidence in the data to suggest that support was more frequently used as praise or approval of adequately functioning families than as a form of encouragement to the less adequately functioning. Speculation as to reasons for this tendency centered on the fact that support in the form of praise and approval was about the only resource other than information which workers saw as appropriate for adequately functioning families, and the workers were possibly preoccupied with instrumentally oriented and directive techniques of intervention at the expense of affective concerns. Our knowledge that effective workers used more and increasing amounts of support with their clients as time went on gives us no clear understanding of how it was used: to praise, to encourage, to approve? Such an understanding could come only through a reanalysis of Treatment Log content from an entirely different perspective. However, as we have noted before in reference to other variables and implied above with regard to the use of support, it does seem clear that relatively more successful workers use some of the same resources more effectively than their less successful colleagues.

Summary and Conclusion

Two classes of findings have been presented regarding patterns of intervention, those that apply across worker caseloads on what we have referred to as the aggregate level, and those that attempt to compare the patterns of intervention em-

ployed by successful or effective workers and their less successful colleagues. Aggregated data related to the temporal
pattern of intervention, the process of resource exchange between worker and client, and the type and mix of resources
exchanged provided preliminary assurance that the treatment
strategy as operationally defined had been executed. In all,
five statistically significant associations were uncovered between intervention variables and change in family functioning
scores or movement. The first such association indicated
that improved family functioning was related to visiting patterns that remained constant rather than increased or decreased
in frequency of contact as time went on. The second indicated improved family functioning was associated with those
clients who actively engaged in the analysis of their own problems. The remaining three statistically significant associations were negatively related to improved family functioning.
They indicated that the greater the amount of direction, analysis, and coordinated service directed from worker to client,
the less likely would be that family's improved functioning.
At the aggregate level of analysis, then, findings could not be
said to have been especially helpful in identifying effective patterns of intervention for replication.

When the full range of intervention variables were examined for rank correlation with worker effectiveness, no significant associations were uncovered. However, a rather traditional profile of casework activity was disclosed by trends in
the data on resources exchanged. They revealed the relatively
more successful worker to be more supportive and less directive, to have provided clients with a greater degree of coordinated community services and increasing amounts of information as time went on, and to have elicited greater client
participation in treatment. Correlational analysis did not give
solid support to any of these findings, and in the end we are
compelled to conclude that the only truly tenable definition of
worker effectiveness revolved around the rate of improvement
in their respective caseloads.

Two reasons for these unremarkable findings can be offered, one relates to the nature of outcome, while the other is
a methodological consideration. The outcome study of FLIP's
interventive efforts--totally separate from the process study
reported in this chapter--indicated that the Project's impact
was less than statistically significant. Although at the time
the process study was undertaken we were unaware of the Project's outcome, we can now, of course, say that the marginal
gains resulting from intervention and the related limited varia-

tion in outcome rates among the bulk of the workers when subjected to our microscopic, and in that sense highpowered, analysis made the discovery of conclusive findings very unlikely.

Although our study of process appears to have accurately monitored most aspects of the treatment strategy it failed to include the use of educational techniques, an activity of considerable emphasis in the treatment program. Its omission is the result of our inability to make a conceptual distinction between information that carried educational content and information that did not. Thus, an extremely important dimension of the treatment strategy--worker mediated, educational experiences--was not tested. Beyond that, however, there is now some reason to believe that a fairly well developed strategy of intervention with continuous in-service training and close supervision cannot by itself produce a successful outcome when you cannot identify the critical qualities of effective worker performance.

Notes

1. Although the original budget provided for the employment of a number of professionally trained workers, a continuous rise in professional salaries during the pre-service phase of the Project left us without the resources to hire trained and competent workers in nontenured positions. A single worker with a master's degree in social work, whom we managed to employ at the start of the action phase, left after a short stay for other employment.

2. For a detailed statement on guidelines for the overall program of intervention, based on a study of several random samples of young urban families including FLIP's, see Geismar, Preventive Intervention in Social Work. See also the section of intervention strategies in this chapter.

3. There was no way of correcting this deficiency in timing short of putting into the field a sizable contingent of skilled interviewers who could complete the first interviewing phase in the shortest possible time, followed by a large treatment staff who would also complete their initial treatment contacts quickly. Given the realities of manpower and training efforts, the above

alternatives were never actually feasible. Data comparing the two types of evaluation--one ranging from
the first interview to the final interview, and the other
from the first treatment contact to the final interview--
indicate that in 135 out of 177 comparisons (76%), some
movement score difference between the two evaluation
periods is present. When change scores were grouped
into five categories--high negative (4 and more scale
steps), low negative (1 to 3 scale steps), zero change,
low positive (1 to 3 scale steps), and high positive
change (4 and more scale steps)--only 68 cases, or
38% of the total, showed a comparison discrepancy
by falling into different categories. Differences were
in both directions, but slightly more families (36 vs.
32) had higher change scores when change was measured over the shorter treatment period. Nevertheless, the basic similarity of both assessments is at-
tested to by a high gamma correlation (16 d. f.) of
+. 75. The correlation is statistically significant beyond the . 001 level (X^2 = 71. 72, 2 d. f.).

4. This program of intervention was originally presented by
    Geismar in <u>Preventive Intervention in Social Work</u>.

5. Of the 95 families lost to the study, 61 refused to con-
    tinue, 27 moved beyond the study area, 6 could not
    be located after initial contacts, and 1 could not be
    continued because of a language barrier (Chinese).

6. Scores are based on nine, rather than eight, areas of
    family functioning. The ninth area, which is not used
    in previous chapters, is Relationship to FLIP worker.

7. Although it might initially seem more appropriate to place
    Child Training Methods under instrumental activities,
    especially when the role of discipline in training is
    considered, the data collected referred overwhelmingly
    to the expressive aspects of the parent-child interac-
    tion related to training.

8. Although Use of Worker was intended as an instrumental
    category, it became evident that what was being eval-
    uated was the behavioral complement of an essentially
    positive attitudinal orientation toward the worker. FLIP
    workers carried out many instrumental tasks while wor
    king with Project families, but their use by the client
    hinged on the way in which the client related to them.

9. This is not inconsistent with the finding presented in
    Chapter 5 that 12% of the study population received
    overall ratings denoting maximum adequacy. The
    12% included only those families who received a 7
    in all major categories.

10. Geismar, op. cit. Passages adopted are included in
    pp. 70 through 80.

11. These levels of functioning were employed in the devel-
    opment of a model of intervention and approximate
    but are not identical to the distinctions in levels of
    functioning used in the analysis.

12. The authors express an intellectual debt to Professor
    Herbert Aptekar for the ideas expressed in this pas-
    sage.

13. Again, the debt to Dr. Aptekar.

14. Charles F. Grosser, "Community Development Programs
    Serving the Urban Poor," Social Work, X, July 1965,
    pp. 15-21.

15. Of particular relevance were the following works: Robert
    F. Bales, Interaction Process Analysis, Cambridge,
    Mass.: Addison-Wesley, 1951; Erika Chance, Fam-
    ilies in Treatment, New York: Basic Books, 1959;
    John C. Glidewell, "On the Analysis of Social Inter-
    vention," in Glidewell (ed.), Parental Attitudes and
    Child Behavior, Springfield, Ill.: Charles C. Thomas,
    1960, pp. 215-239; Norman I. Harway and Howard
    P. Iker, "Computer Analysis of Content in Psycho-
    therapy," in Gary E. Stollak, Bernard G. Guerney,
    and Meyer Rothberg (eds.), Psychotherapy Research,
    Chicago, Ill.: Rand McNally, 1966, pp. 667-669;
    Florence Hollis, "Exploration in the Development of
    a Typology of Casework Treatment," Social Casework,
    XLVIII, June 1967, pp. 335-349, and "The Coding
    and Application of a Typology of Casework Treatment,"
    Social Casework, XLVIII, October 1967, pp. 489-497;
    George Homans, Social Behavior: Its Elementary
    Forms, New York: Harcourt, Brace, and World,
    1961; Henry L. Lennard and Arnold Bernstein, The
    Anatomy of Psychotherapy, New York: Columbia

University Press, 1960; Timothy Leary and Merton
Gill, "The Dimensions and a Measure of the Process
of Psychotherapy: A System for the Analysis of the
Content of Clinical Evaluations and Patient-Therapist
Verbalization," in E. A. Rubinstein and M. B. Par-
loff (eds.), Research in Psychotherapy, Vol. 1, Wash-
ington, D. C.: American Psychological Association,
1959, pp. 62-95; Richard Longabaugh, "A Category
System for Coding Interpersonal Behavior as Social
Exchange," Sociometry, 26, September 1963, pp. 319-
344; Henry J. Meyer, Edgar F. Borgatta, and David
Fanshel, "A Study of the Interview Process: The
Casework-Client Relationship," General Psychological
Monographs, 69, 1964, pp. 247-295; Talcott Parsons
and Robert F. Bales, Family; Socialization and Inter-
action Process, Glencoe, Ill.: Free Press, 1955;
Talcott Parsons and Edward Shils, "The Basic Struc-
ture of the Interactive Relationship," in Parsons and
Shils, Toward A General Theory of Action, Cambridge,
Mass.: Harvard University Press, 1952, pp. 105-
107; Jeanne S. Phillips, Ruth G. Matarozzo, Joseph
D. Matarozzo, George Saslow, and Frederick H. Kan-
fer, "Relationship Between Descriptive Content and
Interaction Behavior in Interviews," Journal of Con-
sulting Psychology, 25, 1961, pp. 260-266; Helen D.
Sargent, "Intraphysic Change: Methodological Prob-
lems in Psychotherapy Research," in Stollak, Guerney,
and Rothberg, op. cit., pp. 14-31; Seattle Atlantic
Street Center Recording System," Seattle Wash., 1964;
Roy P. Wakeman, "Using Data Processing to Analyze
Worker Activity," Social Work Practice 1965, New
York: Columbia University Press, 1965, pp. 54-64;
John W. Thibaut and Harold H. Kelley, The Social
Psychology of Groups, New York: John Wiley, 1959,
p. 12.

16. Longabaugh, op. cit.

17. For citations see Ibid., pp. 319-320.

18. Ibid., p. 322.

19. Ibid., Depriving is subdivided into taking-away and with-
     holding, non-acceptance into ignoring and rejection.

20. The term direction appears more appropriate to the
     client-worker exchange than control because the latter

can connote a pathological relationship within the context of professional nomenclature.

21. See Bruce W. Lagay and Ludwig Geismar, "The Treatment Log - A Recording Procedure for Casework Practice and Research," New Brunswick, N. J.: Graduate School of Social Work, Rutgers University 1966, (mimeographed).

22. See Margaret Blenkner, "Obstacles to Evaluating Research in Casework, Part II," Social Casework, XXXI, March 1950, pp. 97-105; and Howard E. Freeman and Clarence C. Sherwood, Social Research and Social Policy, Englewood Cliffs, N. J.: Prentice-Hall, 1970, pp. 86-89 and 71-72.

23. For a detailed presentation see Bruce Lagay, "A Manual on a Method for Coding Worker-Client Activity in Social Casework," New Brunswick, N. J.: Rutgers Family Life Improvement Project, 1969 (mimeographed).

24. For definitions of modes of exchange, Lagay, "A Manual on a Method for Coding Worker-Client Activity in Social Casework," pp. 7-8.

25. Defined in an earlier section of this chapter as obtaining a score of 4 in one or more areas of functioning.

26. In this section of the analysis the coefficient of contingency (C) rather than gamma was used to measure the association between variables.

27. The apparent conflict between figures referring to "discussants" and figures on pages 45 and 46 relating to "participants" results from the fact that the former enumerates discussants for all subjects discussed over the course of intervention, while the latter is the sum of the appearances of significant others on a week-of-treatment basis. A count of participants tells only how many different people were engaged by the worker, the discussant count is a weighted figure noting relative degrees of participation.

28. Factor analysis as described in footnote on page 64 of Chapter 5 yielded three major factors with a comparable line-up of sub-categories. The factors were

(1) interpersonal-expressive, (2) instrumental, and (3) economic. The major differences between the above conceptualization and the factor groupings were as follows: Role sub-categories, which were most heavily loaded in Column 1 (first factor) composed of sub-categories denoting expressive behavior, became part of this factor termed interpersonal-expressive. The sub-categories under Economic Practices were heavily loaded in Column 3 rather than under Column 2 (factor 2) which is made up of sub-categories identified above as denoting instrumental behavior.

29.   The totals for each period sometimes fall 1 or 2% short of 100% because of the inclusion of "not classified" in the computational scale.

30.   Compare the extensive use of exploration in William J. Reid and Ann W. Shyne, Brief and Extended Casework, New York: Columbia University Press, 1969, p. 91.

31.   The amount of analysis that took place may be understated because communications aimed at defining relationships between actions and their motives which occurred in question and answer form may have been coded at times under information seeking and giving. The distinction is not easily made in every instance.

32.   This figure is arrived at by multiplying the 177 families in the population served by 42, or the mean number of Treatment Logs per family; that product is multiplied by 5, representing the subject units of discussion per week of treatment; and finally, that product is in turn multiplied by 2, representing the number of exchanges per subject unit discussed, yielding a final product of 74,340 exchanges. This figure has been rounded to 70,000 to account for weeks with fewer than five subjects discussed.

Chapter 8

BROADENING THE SCOPE OF EVALUATION

To broaden the scope of our evaluation of Project services, two additional research efforts were undertaken. First the treatment and control groups were compared using so-called hard data, that is, readily verifiable and easily measurable acts, events, or other phenomena that support the premise of desirable change. Secondly, the client reported directly on change as she/he perceived it, a procedure which brought the subject into the evaluation procedure itself.

It is difficult to identify relevant hard data. To a large extent it is a question of agreeing on meaningful hard data criteria which are in line with the goals of the Project. This program of intervention, like those of other social work projects, had as its goal more adequate family functioning which could be translated as better jobs, self-support, less delinquency, fewer out-of-wedlock children, etc. The list is by no means exhaustive. Any one of these results and many others might be seen as a desirable by-product of services. However, in some situations they might be found to be of secondary or decidedly less importance. In addition, it is often difficult to obtain hard data where these are being supplied by an authority over whose method of compilation the investigator has no control.

The problem of defining meaningful hard data criteria and the question of their lack of it with what was considered successful outcome has been discussed elsewhere.[1] As stated above, so-called hard data have been collected here, not because they are inherently more valid than the scale data on social functioning[2] but rather because they are relevant to a full appraisal of changes occurring during the Project period.

Objective data as indices of change. We looked at more than a dozen objective or easily measurable data covering changes in source and amount of income, family structure and composition, incidence of legal deviance, and use of a

range of community resources. The 352 treatment and control families who remained in the Project throughout the entire period were used for this analysis. The data were
documented with the aid of the Profile of Family Functioning [the table in Appendix H shows the complete data
for this analysis].

The results show that both the experimental and control families made limited economic gains, the largest experienced by families headed by unmarried mothers. The
proportion of such mothers who were fully self-supporting increased in the treatment group from 9.5% at the beginning to
30.2% at the end of the Project and in the control group from
5.5% to 25.5%, an overall gain of 20.7% and 20% for treatment and control groups, respectively. In two-parent families there was a very slight gain of 2.7% (from 88.2% at the
beginning to 90.9% at the end) for the treatment group and a
very slight loss of .8% (from 92.3% to 91.5%) for the control
group. Of all families, both one- and two-parent types, who
were not financially independent at the outset of the Project,
30.1% of the treatment group and 25.4% of the control group
were fully self-supporting at the end. The percentage of families earning incomes below $5,000 declined from 42.2% at
the start to 30.7% at the end of the Project for the treatment
group and from 30.4% to 23.1% for the control group, representing a decrease of 11.5% in treatment families and 7.3%
in control families at the lowest income levels. The treatment group enjoyed a slight edge in relative gains over the
control group families, but these were too small to be statistically significant. (Differences between treatment and control groups were less than 5%.)

Looking at family structure and composition we find
the mean number of children born to unmarried mothers by
the end of the study was 1.79 for the treatment group and
2.04 for the control group. The mean number of children
for treatment and control two-parent families was 1.88 and
1.96, respectively. By the end of the Project a higher proportion of unmarried mothers in the control group had married (18.2% control and 11.3% treatment, respectively). Also,
a slightly higher proportion of married parents in the treatment group were divorced or separated at the end of the Project (10% and 8.5%). We note that the slight gain treatment
families made over control families in the economic area is
not repeated in the area of family structure and composition.
Some of the findings are ambiguous; that is, it is difficult
to decide whether they represent desirable or undesirable

change or movement which cannot be so evaluated. Thus, one of the most clear-cut indicators of change is the number of children born to unmarried mothers, while break up of marriage, although widely employed as an index of family stability, represents a more questionable indicator of family functioning. In the first instance the treatment group presented a more desirable change picture; in the second, the control group. However, whatever differences were observed between groups were minimal.

In the area of legal deviance, a very slight rise was observed in the percentage of both treatment and control families in which a member was known to parole or probation services and in which a member was in a penal or other correctional institution. On the first measure the treatment group showed an increase of 2.3% and the control group .7%. On the second measure the proportion of such cases in the treatment group increased by 1.7% and in the control group by .6%. While the control group showed a smaller increase of legal deviance, the differences between the two groups of families were too small to be considered meaningful.

When it came to utilizing agencies, both treatment and control groups showed at the end of the Project an increase in their use of public employment services, OEO programs, recreational facilities, public parks or playgrounds, and private medical facilities. The use of public health facilities decreased slightly. The differences observed between treatment and control families were small (less than 5% in nearly all of the measures). The above data suggest that the use of these facilities and agencies is related to life-cycle factors rather than to FLIP intervention.

All in all, the hard data evidence, lacking, as it does, a firm theoretical basis for making comparisons, shows small differences between treatment and control groups.

Clients' self-evaluation of change. Somewhere near the midpoint of the Project the research investigators decided to expand the evaluation of services by eliciting directly from the client an assessment of the changes that had taken place since participation in the Family Life Improvement Project had begun. The use of direct evaluations by the client as well as the social worker may be viewed as a method of validating the research evaluation reported in prior chapters. It should be stated, nonetheless, that while a measure of agreement among the methods should be anticipated, very close correspondence could not realistically be expected because each one of the evaluative techniques takes a somewhat different manner of viewing a situation.

Although somewhat rare in outcome research the client's perception of his own progress had been considered by several researchers in the social work field. Elizabeth Most[3] conducted a study in which the client's evaluation of marital satisfaction at three periods of time was used to measure change brought about by a marriage counseling service. In another research effort Sacks, Bradley, and Beck[4] compared the views of workers and their clients relative to the latter's progress in a family agency setting. In yet a third study, John Crane, Louis Reimer, and Susan Poulos[5] dealt briefly as a side issue with the relationship between client and worker assessment of movement in a public welfare agency.

At FLIP a structured questionnaire [shown in Appendix I] was designed to elicit the client's own assessment of change. It contained 49 items, and included one or two questions on each of the sub-categories in the family functioning scale. Thus, there were between 4 and 10 questions for each of the 8 areas of functioning. (All areas but Relationship to Worker were included.) Responses were of forced choice ranging from 1 to 5 as follows: The situation is now (1) much worse, (2) slightly worse, (3) no change, (4) slightly better, (5) much better.

At the end of the Project all study families in the experimental and control groups were asked to complete the evaluation form. In addition, all workers completed an identical form for each case. We had originally intended to include both groups in this analysis. However, further consideration led us to entertain serious reservations about the validity of the procedure for families in the control group. Respondents, nearly all mothers, had been instructed to answer the questionnaire by comparing their situations at the end of the Project with the same ones three years earlier, at the time of the first research interview. For the experimental group, or those families who had regular and in-depth contact with a Project worker, the beginning of FLIP services probably constituted a salient point of time. We thought it very likely that they would be able to recall the beginning situation. This was facilitated by the intervention process which frequently involved a review of the earlier situation. On the other hand, the control families had less frequent contact, a lower degree of Project involvement, and a smaller amount of attention focused on their beginning problems and needs. We concluded that it

would be very difficult for these respondents to recall their
family's situation at the start of the research project, and
thus to answer the questionnaire meaningfully. [6] For these
reasons we decided to restrict this analysis to data obtained
from the 177 experimental families. Twenty clients failed to
respond to the structured instrument; thus the findings are
based on 157 treatment families.

Each of the completed questionnaires was assigned a
score[7] for each area of family functioning and overall functioning, representing a given client's evaluation of whether
the situation had improved, remained the same, or had deteriorated.

The data pertaining to the client's assessment of
changes in overall functioning and in the areas of family functioning are shown in Table 16.

The table shows that the bulk of clients (77. 7%) considered overall changes which had occurred in their family
situation since the start of their participation in FLIP to have
been of a positive nature. With the exception of a single
client (representing . 6% of the clients) none reported that
their situation had become worse; and the remaining clients
(21. 7%) felt that their situation had not changed. Most of the
clients who indicated that positive change had occurred reported it to be of a limited amount (65. 6% fell into the category of lesser positive change and 12. 1% into the category of
greater positive change). The view of overall change as presented by the client differs from that emerging from the Profile ratings, with a higher proportion of the self-evaluations
registering positive change (77. 7% compared to 48. 6%) [see
Table 8, Chapter 6]. In the clients' evaluation there is an
almost complete absence of overall negative change (. 6%) but
in the Profile ratings over one-third (38. 4%) of the clients
exhibited negative movement. [8] The clients' assessment showed
relatively more "no changers" than did the Profile measurement (21. 7% compared to 13. 0%).

For the most part (see Table 16) a pattern similar to
that observed for overall functioning was found for the main
categories of functioning. In all areas but Health Conditions
and Practices a majority of clients reported that positive
change had taken place with percentages ranging from 39. 8%
to 82. 0% for the eight categories of functioning, the mean
percent being equal to 65. 1. Excluding the area of Economic
Practices, a larger proportion of clients indicated "lesser

Table 16. Percentage Distribution of Clients
Based on Self-Evaluation of Movement
for Main Categories and Overall Functioning

Area	Negative Change (Mean scores 1.0-2.7)	No Change (Mean scores 2.8-3.2)	Lesser Positive Change (Mean scores 3.3-3.9)	Greater Positive Change (Mean scores 4.0-5.0)	%	Total Number
Family Relationships & Unity	5.8	26.9	42.9	24.4	100.0	156
Individual Behavior & Adjustment	1.3	18.6	42.3	38.7	100.0	156
Care & Training of Children	1.3	29.5	43.6	25.6	100.0	156
Social Activities	4.5	44.8	35.3	15.4	100.0	156
Economic Practices	10.9	7.1	32.7	49.3	100.0	156
Home & Household Practices	3.8	21.8	43.0	31.4	100.0	156
Health Conditions & Practices	7.7	52.5	24.4	15.4	100.0	156
Use of Community Resources	5.1	37.8	49.4	7.7	100.0	156
Total Score	.6	21.7	65.6	12.1	100.0	157

*The total number of 156 instead of 157 for each area of functioning because, in each of the areas, answers were missing for a single respondent.

positive change" than "greater positive change," while the reverse is true for the economic category.

A negative change is noted by 1.3% to 10.9% of the clients for the eight areas of functioning, the mean percent being equal to 5.1%. No change is indicated by 7.1% to 52.5% of the clients, with the mean at 29.9%.

By assigning weights of 1 - 4 to the four levels of movement, we derived a weighted score[9] for each area of functioning that permitted the ranking of areas according to degree of improvement perceived by the client. As shown below in the first column of Table 17, the two areas of greatest improvement from the perspective of the client were Economic Conditions and Practices, and Individual Behavior and Adjustment. The least amount of improvement was found in the two areas of Health Conditions and Practices, and Use of Community Resources.

Various efforts to explain the rank order obtained proved unrewarding. We considered the possibility that, relative to positive change, the position of an area might depend on whether it was one of predominantly instrumental or expressive functioning. Inspecting the first column of Table 17, it is clear that no such pattern was found. Areas characterized predominantly by instrumental functioning (Economic Practices, Care and Training of Children, Home and Household Practices, Health Conditions and Practices, and Use of Community Resources) occupied top, middle, and bottom positions. Similarly, Individual Behavior and Adjustment, Social Activities, and Family Relationships--areas of predominantly expressive functioning--were at the top and bottom of the rank order.

There was always the possibility that clients might see greater improvement in those areas that were characterized by greater problemicity at the beginning. However, when the rank orders of the areas on the two dimensions (improvement as seen by client and adequacy of beginning functioning based on the profile) were correlated, no relationship was found.

The finding that clients viewed Individual Behavior and Adjustment as a category in which considerable improvement took place is not unexpected, for this is an area in which the clients' subjective feelings figure prominently and one in which they are likely to be aware of subtle changes in feeling states.

Table 17. Rank Order of Areas According to
Movement Based on Client Self-Evaluation and Profile Ratings*

Area	Weighted Score Movement According to Client Self-Assessment	Rank	Weighted Score Movement According to Profile Ratings	Rank
Econ. Condit. & Practices	320.4	1	305.2**	4
Indiv. Behav. & Adjustment	316.6	2	301.7	5
Home/Household Practices	302.0	3	325.4	1
Care/Training of Children	293.5	4	278.6	8
Family Relationships & Unity	285.9	5	298.5	6
Soc. Activities	261.6	6	313.5	2
Community Resources Use	259.7	7	306.0	3
Health Condit. & Practices	247.5	8	298.4	7

Spearman rank order correlation = +.143

*The higher the score the more positive the outcome.

**Following the procedure described in 10 these scores
were obtained using the percentages given in Table 9, Chapter 6.

We explored the degree of correspondence between the relative position of the areas of functioning derived from the client's self-assessment and that based on the Profile measurements. Following a procedure similar to that employed in ranking areas according to the client's evaluation, we ordered the categories of functioning according to degree of positive change based on the profile measurements[10] and correlated the two rank orders. A very low and statistically nonsignificant correlation was observed, pointing to a virtual absence of correspondence between the two perceptions of movement. (The weighted scores and ranks derived from the two measures of change are shown in Table 17.)

We compared the data on the assessment of movement by FLIP clients with the findings of the study by Sacks and his colleagues.[11] The effort was complicated by the fact that the two studies approached client self-evaluation in different ways. Overall change in this study was derived from the clients' responses to all the questionnaire items. In the Sack's study "global assessment" was determined by asking the client a single general question about change. Moreover, the areas of family functioning in the study by Sacks et al. differed from those in the FLIP study, and the methods of computing change indices were dissimilar. If we can assume that the differences in method of analysis did not affect the substantive results of the studies, we can conclude that both studies agreed that the majority of clients believed improvement had taken place and only a very small proportion thought that deterioration had occurred.[12]

Let us return now to the question of the compatibility of the client's evaluation of change with other methods of assessing movement. The lack of correspondence between self-evaluation scores and those produced by Profile ratings, noted above, was based on an overall rather than a case-by-case comparison. However, the latter type of analysis was also carried out, and involved a study of the congruence in assessment of change between client questionnaires, social worker questionnaires (similar to those of the client), and the Profile of Family Functioning. This analysis is reported in Appendix J.

Findings of this last analysis, i.e., a comparison of three methods of evaluation on a case-by-case basis, revealed a greater degree of compatibility among the various modes of assessing movement than that which the overall comparison of clients' self-evaluations with Profile ratings yielded. Positive

relationships of moderate strength were found between both
clients' and workers' evaluations of change (based on the
structured instrument) and Profile ratings of change. The
comparison of clients' and workers' responses to the structured questionnaire showed extensive agreement.

Though these findings, based on a case-by-case analysis, may be said to provide a more rigorous test of comparability and thereby furnish a small measure of validation for
the techniques of evaluation, they fail to supply convincing
evidence of positive outcome. While dismissing, as we did
for reasons discussed earlier, experimental control group
comparisons on self-evaluation, we are in no position to state
that the seemingly favorable picture reflected in the attitudes
of the treatment group mothers (Table 16) truly denotes positive outcome. Attitudes expressed, it would seem, bring together a variety of perceived influences on the lives of the
young families, not the least of which might be the built-in
optimism of the young, affirming faith in an idea that as the
family grows, things are getting better. The effects of Project intervention are likely to play a part in this assessment, [13]
but to those must be added change in the general social and
economic situation, change in family fortunes that are independent of the intervention program, and many, many other
factors. Though we may discount control group self-evaluation
data as not strictly comparable and valid, their similarity to
those of the treatment group [see note 6] would suggest that
similar psychological mechanisms are operating in the evaluations of both groups. This conclusion, then, and the evidence supplied by the so-called objective change indices leads
us to terminate the present chapter on a note stressing the
substantial difficulties confronting efforts to marshal multi-
dimensional and valid evidence about the progress of a program of social intervention.

Notes

1.   Geismar and Krisberg, op. cit., pp. 354-369.

2.   For a full discussion of this issue see Leonard S. Kogan
      and Ann Shyne, "Tender-Minded and Tough-Minded
      Approaches in Evaluative Research," Welfare in Re-
      view, Vol. 4, No. 2, February 1966, pp. 12-17.

3.   Elizabeth Most, "Measuring Change in Marital Satisfac-
      tion," Social Work, Vol. 9, No. 3, July 1964, pp.
      64-70.

4. Joel G. Sacks, Panke M. Bradley, and Dorothy Fahs
   Beck, Client's Progress Within Five Interviews,
   Family Service Association of America, New York,
   1970, pp. 52-81.

5. John Crane, Louis Reimer, and Susan Poulos, An Experiment in the Deployment of Welfare Aides, Research Department Children's Aid Society of Vancouver, British Columbia, June 1970, p. 27.

6. A comparison of questionnaire responses by experimental
   and control group mothers showed virtually identical
   results in respondents' evaluation of change when mean
   scores were compared. Control group responses
   were positive on more items, treatment group responses were more intensely positive. For details
   see Geismar, Gerhart, Lagay, op. cit., pp. 122-124.

7. The following procedure was employed in developing the
   score. It will be recalled that the answer to any
   given item ranged from much worse to much better
   and was represented by numbers 1 to 5, respectively.
   The mean score for a given area of functioning was
   obtained by summing the numbers symbolizing the
   responses for all items comprising that area and then
   dividing by the number of items answered. If an
   item was left unanswered by the respondent or if the
   response was "not applicable", this item was omitted
   from the calculations. A total score was derived in
   the same manner. Numbers representing all answered
   items were summed scores ranged from 1 to 5 and
   cut-off points for defining change were selected as
   follows: 1.0 - 2.7 Negative change
              2.8 - 3.2 No Change
              3.3 - 3.9 Lesser positive change
              4.0 - 5.0 Greater positive change

8. Consideration should be given to the possibility that
   clients who did not respond to the questionnaire felt
   that negative movement had occurred.

9. Weights of 1 - 4 were assigned in ascending order from
   negative movement to no change, lesser positive movement, and greater positive movement, respectively.
   For each area of functioning the appropriate weight
   was multiplied by the percentage of clients falling
   into each level of movement and the four figures
   were summed to obtain the total weighted score.

10. The ranking of areas according to movement measured
     by profile ratings was accomplished by using a
     weighted score for each area of functioning. The
     score, obtained in a manner similar to that described
     earlier, for determining the score representing the
     clients' self-evaluation of change, involved assigning
     weights of 1 to 5 to the five levels of movement
     ("high negative" to "high positive", respectively), by
     the appropriate weight, and summing these figures.

11. Sacks et al. , op. cit. , pp. 52-64.

12. Ibid.

13. When asked specifically about the effect of Project ser-
     vices on the life of their families, 79% of the clients
     checked mainly positive effects, 16.4% indicated that
     the services made no difference, 2.6% listed positive
     and negative effects, and 2% cited mainly negative
     effects.   Geismar, Gerhart, and Lagay, op. cit. ,
     p. 124.

Chapter 9

OUTCOME RESEARCH AND SOME IMPLICATIONS
FOR SERVICE PLANNING

The Family Life Improvement Project, reported in the
foregoing pages, represented an effort to rigorously evaluate
a program of social work intervention. The undertaking was
inspired by the firm conviction that methods of practice must
be tested by assessing outcome. Being evaluated was a program of intervention combining quasi-traditional and innovative
approaches to helping families. The innovative aspect resided
in offering services to a random sample of young families, a
group whose functioning was reasonably adequate so that the
need for immediate aid was confined to a decided minority.
Based on the theoretical notion, partly supported by control
group data, that young families move toward greater malfunctioning as they grow older, a program of intervention was
offered to the treatment group with the expectation that positive outcome would mean successful prevention. The program
of services relied heavily upon social casework, with major
emphasis on situational intervention and individualized patterns
of helping which were geared to a family's own level of social functioning. Because most of the families were non-
problematic, a good deal of social worker activity was directed
toward enhancing social functioning (rather than problem solv-
ing) with a concentration on such instrumental aspects as employment, education and job training, housing, health, family
planning, etc.

Results of the program, described in some detail in
Chapters 6 to 8, could be termed as only partially supporting
the major intervention hypothesis which postulated significantly
more positive movement in the experimental group than in the
control group. In fact, treatment families showed significantly
more positive change than control cases in only three out of
eight areas--Child Care and Training, Health Conditions and
Practices, and Home and Household Practices. In four other
areas experimental cases had a slight edge over control cases,
and in one, the reverse was true.

Refinement of the outcome analysis by examining the
effect of family background variables on treatment results
showed that services were particularly helpful to families who
functioned either well or poorly at the start of the Project,
to lower-class families who functioned at an adequate level
when the program began, and to units where the mother grew
up in a highly malfunctioning family but whose own family
functioned quite well when services began. The last two categories represent families presenting a latent factor predis-
posing them toward malfunctioning, as was shown in Chapter
5. This raises a new question. Are families who have overcome obstacles of the past more responsive to help than those
without such an experience?

In a detailed analysis of service input, the social worker emerges as a more important outcome variable than the
substantial number of treatment resources and intervention
patterns examined. The relatively more successful worker
was found to have been supportive rather than directive, to
have shown accelerated efforts toward providing information
and coordinated community services, and to have elicited
greater client participation in treatment.

The Family Life Improvement Project is one of a
growing number of research projects in social work which
have sought to test the results of professional intervention by
means of an adequate experimental-control design. The goal
in FLIP, as in any other evaluation study, is to generalize
from the findings which have been produced. The chances of
arriving at some valid generalizations are greater when this
Project is put into context with other studies resembling it
in at least some respects. This is seen as a second best
effort to direct replication, which is obviously not a possibility. Thus, before resuming the discussion on the results of
the Family Life Improvement Project and raising the question
of policy implications, we shall extend consideration to some
of the evaluation research referred to above.

Results of Other Social Work Outcome Studies. In
Chapter 2 reference has been made to some eight outcome
studies, other than the present one, dealing with programs
of intervention in family life. As stated earlier, these studies
do not replicate one another, nor are they planned as part of
an overall design for testing one or more common hypotheses.
Yet, collectively or by sub-groups, these projects present
some common denominators with respect to method of intervention and instruments of measurement. Thus, it is pos-

sible to examine outcome relative to certain input variables, although the comparisons will need to be accompanied by certain reservations arising from the small number of cases and the absence of an overall, comprehensive design.

As a beginning step it is necessary to state the ground rules for inclusion in the comparison. First, like the Family Life Improvement Project, all the studies selected represent programs of intervention dealing with total families rather than individuals. In treatment modalities, service objectives, and the criteria chosen for evaluating the attainment of goals, family-focused services differ from those which are aimed at helping the individual. Secondly, these are studies in which the effects of more-or-less clearly defined programs of intervention are compared with those resulting from a situation in which no treatment or service was rendered, or where services were standard and routine in character and limited in scope (such as the run-of-the-mill public assistance services) so as to constitute--from the point of view of the special service program objectives--the equivalent of a no treatment situation.[1]

Third, the studies listed utilized an experimental-control design whereby cases were assigned to their respective groups in a manner which assured the similarity of relevant characteristics at inception. This is generally accomplished by the use of matching or randomizing techniques. Fourth, evaluation of outcome was carried out with the aid of objectively verifiable criteria and/or the use of tested instruments of measurement. Fifth, numbers in the experimental and control groups were 30 or larger. And sixth, each one of the studies specified the major service objectives in advance, against which actual results could be judged at termination of the treatment phase.

The writers do not claim that the roster of studies dealt with here represents a comprehensive list of those meeting the six above-mentioned specifications. These are the ones which have been publicized in the North American social work literature. Others which have not received publicity or appear in the foreign literature may have been overlooked because a systematic canvassing of all possible sources did not seem feasible. At the same time, it should be emphasized that the bulk of the outcome studies, both published and unpublished, do not meet minimum conditions of scientific process. In 1962 Joseph Lagey and Beverly Ayres, after surveying 143 community projects serving multi-problem families, concluded that:

> few projects are employing standardized
> 'objective' measurement scales.   Fewer
> still are employing control groups and
> rare are the projects which use a before-
> after design with a control group. [2]

Most social work outcome studies surveyed by us were
demonstration projects designed to show that a new approach
to serving clients constitutes a contribution to practice.   Samples were generally small, and cases were selected in a hap-
hazard manner.   More often than not, control groups were
absent.   Where the principal investigator sought to provide
evidence of changes in attitudes and behavior, information
was generally lacking about the reliability and validity of the
instruments of measurement.

The nine studies that are being compared here contrast
favorably with dozens of others not cited.   They meet the criteria enumerated above.   They utilized tested instruments of
measurement or new ones that either had obvious face validity
or else, subjected to reliability tests, were found to measure
up to acceptable standards.   Despite these safeguards, and
this point cannot be emphasized too strongly, none of these
studies attained a level of methodological perfection.   Evaluative research which is highly dependent on external conditions
makes tremendous methodological and administrative demands
upon the investigator. [3]   In even the most rigorous of studies,
some compromise on principles of design and method is required to make the research possible.   The adequate study,
in the final analysis, is the one in which basic tenets of research, such as sample comparability, objectivity in measurement, and bias control, have not been violated.

This review does not attempt to furnish a detailed
analysis or critique of these research endeavors.   The goal
is not to expose the strengths and weaknesses of the studies
cited--the interested reader can go to the sources and carry
out whatever analysis best serves the purposes of his own
investigation--but rather to furnish enough information about
each one so that the reader can draw conclusions on outcome
as it relates to relevant research variables.

The common denominator in all the studies was the
use of social casework as the primary method of intervention,
although in two of the studies, the New Haven Neighborhood

Improvement Project (NIP)[4] and the Vancouver Area Development Project (ADP)[5] a variety of other social work methods
and techniques were employed. If we are to define casework
broadly enough to comprehend every one of the approaches
under that label, we can state that it is a process by which
a professional (or a small team of professionals) seek to enhance the social functioning of individuals and families with
the aid of a variety of techniques, generally including study,
diagnosis, treatment planning, interviews with individuals or
small groups of persons having a significant relationship to
each other, work with collaterals (institutions and agencies
that have a bearing on the client's functioning), and evaluation
of services. These are merely the most commonly encountered components of the casework method. In recent years,
largely in response to the needs of population groups that
have not been reached in the past, other techniques--such as
non-verbal interaction, mediation, and advocacy--have been
incorporated.

Unfortunately, these nine projects do not present us
with a uniform approach to casework but with a variety of
patterns of service, differing in the frequency of contact,
number of family members seen, amount of home visiting,
extent to which community resources were used, areas of
treatment emphasized, etc. As to the nature of the casework which was carried out, we are left in most instances
to infer its actual character from the written service objectives. Except for FLIP, which carried out a more detailed
analysis of treatment, and the Midway study, which described
the administrative patterns for the services, the reports on
the research-action projects confined themselves to a brief
description of service patterns or to a statistical accounting
of but a few of the service activities, such as length of service, total and average number of contacts, family members
seen, place of contact, and initiator of contact (Chemung
County Study). [6]

As casework-centered projects, most of the studies
sought to define goals of intervention and measure outcome
in terms of changes in observed behavior, attitudes, adjustment, social functioning, and related concepts, all denoting
the families' mode of adaptation to their environment. Most
of the projects also used evaluation criteria that were multi-
dimensional. That is to say, the concept of measurement
comprised two or more properties. In addition to the main
casework-focused outcome variable, several projects utilized
secondary criteria of success or failure, such as changes in

economic dependency, deviant behavior, etc.   One study alone,
the Delaware Rehabilitation of Dependent Families Project,[7]
evaluated the impact of intensive casework solely in terms of
reduction of economic dependence on public assistance.

As a first step in an effort to view treatment outcome
within the context of nine separate research endeavors, we
are presenting a brief summary of each study (FLIP has been
dealt with in detail) describing objectives, service patterns,
sample, mode of measurement, and major findings. More
detailed information is available in the sources cited and in
unpublished reports on which the published write-ups were
based. The first four studies dealt with specially selected,
severely disorganized--often referred to as multi-problem--
client populations; the subsequent four projects provided services to economically deprived families, known to local public
welfare agencies but not necessarily characterized by social
disorganization.

(1) The Vancouver Area Development Project (ADP)[8]
was a multi-service endeavor offering a coordinated program
of casework, group work, and neighborhood services including
recreational activities and community organization to a group
of 92 specially selected, seriously disorganized families in
the city of Vancouver, British Columbia, Canada. A matched
group of 122 families, randomly assigned as controls, was
not given the special, integrated services but used only the
resources usually available in the community.

The expectation was that integrated services, which
hopefully allow a client family to be treated with reference
to their multiple problems and needs, would result in better
social functioning at the end of the treatment period (about
two years) than the ordinary, fragmented services offered by
the community. The five social workers employed by the
project, loaned by the agencies that participated in this community sponsored program, carried caseloads of twenty families each. Other project workers served in a variety of
professional roles. They directed neighborhood services,
organized and directed recreational and social action groups,
coordinated community services, etc. About half the workers
had master's degrees in social work; the remainder were
college graduates with a major in social work (They had received the B. S. W. , a Canadian degree). All of them had
had prior experience in public welfare, child welfare, or
mental retardation, and they were supervised by a trained
professional with ten years of experience in public welfare
and related fields.

Results of services which were evaluated with the aid
of the St. Paul Scale for Measuring Family Functioning
showed--on the basis of before-and-after measurement--that
integrated services generally proved to be more effective than
usual agency service in modifying the family functioning of
multi-problem families.[9] In five out of eight areas of func-
tioning--Care and Training of Children, Economic Practices,
Home and Household Practices, Health Conditions and Practices, Use of Community Resources--the experimental group
recorded significantly greater positive changes (at .05 level
or beyond) than the control group.

(2) The New Haven Neighborhood Improvement Project
(NIP),[10] like ADP, was a multi-service enterprise and oper-
ated--at least initially[11]--as an alliance of community agencies. In contrast to ADP, NIP was geographically limited to
one area, a low-cost housing project, extending a variety of
services to the residents. The target population was made
up of the 30 most problematic families, and they were the
recipients of intensive, reaching-out casework. However,
other programs and services, such as open-door casework
(a kind of information, counselling, and referral service),
a pre-nursery school, a sports and recreation program for
youth, social, recreational, and service activities for parents
and senior citizens, were offered not only to the problem families but to the other tenants in the housing project as well.
The goal of the research was to evaluate the effects of the
multiple service endeavor upon the thirty disorganized families.

Both trained and untrained workers were employed by
the project, but after an initial turnover--due to the with-
drawal of several agencies--the latter predominated. The
action program and the supervision of casework were in the
hands of a professionally trained, highly experienced caseworker. Full caseloads were pegged at 12 families, although
some workers, employed part-time, carried fewer cases.

The main outcome measure of the study was the social
functioning of families as assessed by the St. Paul Scale.
The functioning of the 30 target families was compared with
that of a control group of 51 similarly selected, seriously
disorganized families residing in other low-cost housing projects in New Haven. The research evaluation, taking the form
of panel interviewing of treatment and control families, covered
an 18 month period. Results showed that there was significantly greater movement in the experimental group when compared to the control group. Greater positive change was

registered in all areas of family functioning, but it was most pronounced in Health Conditions and Practices, Relationship to Social Worker, Use of Community Resources, and Family Relationships and Unity. Treatment families registered an average gain in total score of nearly seven scale steps (+6.93) as compared to .77 of a scale step for the control group.

(3) The Chemung County Research Demonstration with Multi-Problem Families[12] had as its objective the assessment of the effect of intensive social casework on 50 multi-problem families known to the County Welfare Department. These families were selected randomly out of a sample pool of 150 families. The second 50 cases were assigned to a first control group that was given normal public assistance services. The intensive services were rendered within the framework of public assistance policies and procedures by two caseworkers with graduate degrees and prior field experience. A second, after-only control group of 50 families was interviewed and measured at the end of the project only in order to discover the possible effects resulting from the interviewing process. The median length of treatment was 98 weeks. The smaller caseload of demonstration group workers as compared to that of regular County Welfare workers permitted more client contacts, more home visits, and more reaching-out activity by the social worker in the experimental group.

Before-and-after evaluation was carried out by means of the St. Paul Scale; movement in treatment and control families was also assessed with the aid of the Community Service Society (Hunt-Kogan) Scale for the measurement of movement in casework. Both these instruments, which in the framework of this project had been subjected to extensive reliability and validity testing, showed substantially the same results: the demonstration group showed a small but statistically non-significant margin of improvement over the control group.

(4) The Family Center Project of Copenhagen[13] represented an experiment in which social workers under the leadership of a psychologist gave services during a two year period to 70 seriously disorganized families residing in a lower-class area of Copenhagen. A control group of 70 so-called "social twins," families matched to the first for sex and age of head of household, education, number of children, and types of problems, received social support through the customary channels of service. Each family in the set of twins was assigned randomly to one group or the other. The

program of intervention put major emphasis upon "helpful guidance of the activities of the families, especially coordination of their dealings with other social agencies and the solution of their most pressing problems."[14] Problems dealt with most actively were attitudes toward children, social agencies, employment and health, and the proper child care facilities for working mothers.[15] The basic study hypothesis was that the families served by the Center would "manage better and make greater progress than the control group."[16]

The Danish families in this project had fewer children than the multi-problem families in most American projects, but at the same time were marked by a seemingly greater degree of deviance. For instance, 46% of the men and 13% of the women had prison records. Nine-tenths of the families had been in contact with public assistance (despite a low unemployment rate among heads of households) and child welfare, and conflict among adults and children was widespread.

Outcome measurement of the before-and-after type was based on a rating of the functioning in 11 areas of family life. The researchers found moderate improvement spread over most areas of social functioning, but major improvement was registered only in employment and housing. Least movement was registered in psychological problems. When the total movement for the experimental group was compared with that of the control group families, the former showed greater improvement at the 7% level of statistical significance (in other words, the difference was not significant at the 5% level).

(5) The Franklin County, Ohio Experimental Study to Measure the Effectiveness of Casework Service[17] sought to determine whether casework services enable public assistance clients to achieve better psychological and social well-being. The principal investigator assumed that such well-being is a prerequisite for taking advantage of employment opportunities; however, the study did not include provisions for employment since this was viewed as being outside the responsibility of public assistance. This research was designed to compare the effects of intensive casework upon a sample of public assistance clients with the routine service ordinarily provided by the public assistance agency. Intensive casework was defined merely in terms of caseload, the assumption being that small caseloads during a 15-month period of service would allow more contacts, greater individualization of service, and more extensive activity on behalf of each

client. In this study a small caseload consisted of about 50 cases, approximately half the size of the usual public assistance load.

The study sample was composed of 400 public assistance clients, 70% of whom were families, who lived in Franklin County, Ohio. Cases were assigned to experimental and control groups through a matching procedure utilizing 12 demographic and service factors. The four caseworkers who were chosen for the experimental group were selected on the basis of their representativeness of the total staff of public assistance workers.

Since the main focus of the research was on psychosocial and physical well-being, the CSS (Hunt-Kogan) Scale was chosen as the main criterion of measurement. The researcher postulated, nonetheless, some minor hypotheses which anticipated a reduction in economic dependency as a result of the intensive services. The findings strongly supported the major hypothesis of significantly greater movement or improvement of a social and psychological nature in the experimental group. Contrary to expectations, more movement was also found to be significantly associated with greater relief cost and a greater number of cases receiving assistance in the treatment group.

(6) The Community Service Society - Department of Social Services Study (CSS-DSS)[18] brought together a leading private agency with a public agency in New York City in an effort to determine "the effectiveness of this collaborative approach in preventing further individual and family disorganization and in rehabilitating families toward independent economic and psycho-social functioning."[19] The study design utilized a coordinated approach in which DSS supplied income maintenance while CSS provided a wide range of other services needed by the families.

An experimental group of 105 families and a control group of 68 families, all cases known to the Department of Social Services, were studied for a 14 month period. Cases were assigned randomly from the caseloads of a number of district centers in New York City. Experimental group families received the collaborative services of a public assistance worker and a professionally trained CSS caseworker. Five CSS workers served project cases, but when turnovers are counted, about four times that number were involved at one time or another. The median length of employment was 13 months.

Results of services were measured by a specially
devised questionnaire which collected information on the family's social functioning under ten conceptual headings. Interviews which were conducted 14 months after a family's initial
service contact represented, for the most part, the client's
assessment of changes in various areas of social functioning
which had taken place during the treatment period. A comparison of experimental and control groups revealed few significant differences in functioning on the various outcome variables which were studied.

(7) The Chicago Midway Study,[20] a joint endeavor
by the School of Social Service Administration of the University of Chicago and the Cook County Department of Public
Aid, aimed at bettering client functioning by upgrading worker
performance and improving the utilization of social welfare
manpower and the delivery and quality of services. Toward
that end the directors of the study developed a research design
for testing four patterns of service delivery: the conventional
work group form of organization based on the traditional
worker-supervisor relationship; the experimental team operating as a more autonomous unit, with greater specialization
of team members, and restructured responsibilities of workers
and supervisors. Each of these two types of work organization employed Plan A and Plan B of service; Plan A, with
a caseload of 90 per worker, concentrated supervision on
financial need and crisis situations and only residually on
counselling and rehabilitation; Plan B, with a caseload of
45, focused supervision (rendered by a person with a master's
degree in social work) not only on financial assistance but
also on a broad range of services needed by the client. Cases
were assigned to their respective groups by a randomizing
procedure.

Including the Midway Study in our review of the other
outcome studies creates a problem, for here we are not comparing an experimental group with an untreated group, or
even a group served in conventional ways (as was the case
in the Chemung County and Franklin County Projects). Both
Plan A and Plan B represent modifications of the original
service patterns,[21] although the latter is much more far
reaching in its structure and objectives. It can be stated,
however, that both the conventional work group and Plan A
come closer to representing a status quo condition than the
experimental team or Plan B.

We will address ourselves here only to that part of

the Midway Study report which is relevant to our review of outcome research, i. e., the effect of services on 163 project families. [22]

This effect was measured by means of a specially designed schedule which covered 18 areas of individual and family functioning. The schedules were rated for social functioning at the beginning and end of the study and for change during the treatment period, which, for the cases evaluated and reported in the published article, lasted about one year. Results of the study showed that in both Plans A and B, families served by experimental teams did better in items relating to children, in the relational and adjustment and other area classifications than families served by conventional work groups. Only in the adult areas in Plan A and the Household areas in Plan B did families served by conventional work groups do better than their counterparts. One of the most striking changes favoring experimental group families was found in Plan B under items relating to adults. Total scores revealed statistically significantly[23] greater movement for families receiving team services when results of Plans A and B were combined and under Plan A, but not Plan B, when these were rated separately. When families in both conventional work groups and experimental teams were examined together, it was found that those in Plan B showed more overall movement than those in Plan A. Both the team form of service delivery and a reduction in caseload were found to yield better results than the more traditional forms of service; when the two were combined the results were enhanced. However, team organization was found to produce more benefits than the more costly caseload reduction.

(8) The Delaware Rehabilitation of Dependent Families Project[24] investigated the hypothesis that public assistance recipients who receive casework service will become more independent of public assistance and socially and psychologically more stable. The cases analyzed in the study were a stratified random sample of 314 families receiving services in the AFDC program of New Castle County, Delaware. Experimental and control cases were matched on public assistance category (AFDC and AFDC-UP), race, marital status and assigned randomly to one group or the other. Control cases were served by one of the regular agency caseworkers carrying a caseload of 175. Experimental group cases were assigned to one of three workers in a special services unit where the caseload was 35 families. Two years was the duration of the project, but cases were closed as

treatment objectives were attained and replacements were obtained from a common sample pool.

A schedule developed by the Project covered information on demographic data, public assistance characteristics,
family functioning, employment, housing, and mobility of
parents. Additional information on the families was supplied
by content analysis of case records. The research design
utilized the panel study technique, with the interviews covering three time periods: 12-month pre-project, treatment,
follow-up of up to 18 months. [25]

At the time of follow-up a significantly larger percentage of special service families as compared to control
group families (45% vs. 35%) had become independent of public assistance. Significantly more of the former than the
latter remained independent of public assistance during 80%
of the follow-up period. However, the same proportion of
families in both groups, slightly more than one-third, remained on public assistance throughout the follow-up period.
The special services extended to experimental group families
were not found to have had any significant effect upon the
marital status or the social functioning of the recipients.

FLIP and Eight Other Outcome Projects:
An Interpretation

The efficacy of professional intervention cannot be
proved or disproved by the results of these nine outcome
studies testing the effects of social work intervention. However, they furnish far better indicators of results than the
countless poorly planned and executed studies or the intuitive
program evaluations which appear to be the norm in most
agency practice.

The cumulative evidence of these nine endeavors
would tend to deal a decisive blow to two widespread though
diametrically opposed myths: one, that social work is the
answer to the difficulties faced by urban families; the other,
that social work--particularly social casework--is useless as
a means of helping families with their problems. In the
light of the evidence supplied by these nine studies, both
statements are meaningless. Their very generality precludes
a testing of their validity. If the statements were to read
instead that any and all kinds of social work intervention are
useful or useless in dealing with any and all types of family
problems, then it could be said that the collective research

evidence supports neither statement. What, then, are the
conclusions which can be drawn from the completed studies
before us when we formulate our questions more specifically
and therefore more meaningfully?

The outcome registered by the nine action-research
projects ranges from successful to unsuccessful, if we view
results in terms of the objectives defined by the principal investigators. It may be somewhat hazardous to classify results by degree of success because outcome criteria differed
with regard to levels of expectation and also because the researchers did not invariably make the nature of all their research hypotheses clear. Allowing for a measure of inaccuracy in the categorization of outcome, it is, nonetheless,
possible to determine whether or not the basic hypotheses
of each study were supported by the results.

By using the criteria suggested here as well as the
conclusions of the investigators, two projects, The Chemung
County Demonstration and the CSS-DSS Study, could be labeled
as having registered largely negative outcome. [26] Four studies,
New Haven (NIP), Vancouver ADP, the Franklin County Study,
and the Delaware Study, could be categorized as having
achieved a largely positive outcome. The remaining three,
the Copenhagen Family Center Study, the Chicago Midway
Study, and FLIP, could be classified as having shown mixed
outcome, which is to say that some of their objectives were
attained but not others.

With this categorization as a starting point, we are
now able to examine possible correlates of outcome. All
projects but one, the Delaware Study, use changes in client
functioning, adjustment, attitudes, and related variables as
major outcome criteria. While also concerned with changes
in family functioning, the Delaware researcher decided to
make change in the clients' economic dependency status the
major dependent variable. The remaining principal investigators generally selected one or more public assistance status variables as subsidiary indicants of change but affirmed
that they were not the primary objectives of social work
intervention. John Behling clarified the issue most succinctly
by pointing out that social work intervention is designed to
help individuals attain sufficient psychological and physical
well-being to take advantage of employment, but that the provision of employment opportunity lies outside the agency offering social work services. [27] Geismar and Krisberg also
reported changes in the public support of clients but raised

the question of whether reduction in economic dependency is
a valid criterion of movement. [28] Since none of the projects
contained well developed economic rehabilitation programs or
had much influence on the economic opportunity structure,
the general lack of change in dependency status is not surprising. The notable exception is the Delaware Project where
casework service focused on economic rehabilitation seemingly
resulted in a significant rise in families who became independent of public assistance. Casework studies which evaluate changes in economic dependency status, including those
reported here, indicate that treatment of poor people involves
a better assessment of economic need and this, during the
initial stages of service at least, leads to greater, not less,
dependency. [29]

Changes in family functioning, whether measured by
the CSS Scale, the St. Paul Scale, or some newly designed
instrument, were characteristically associated with four programs of social work service. Movement was most pronounced
in the two multi-service projects (ADP and NIP) and two reasonably well integrated casework-public assistance endeavors
(Franklin County and Delaware Studies). In contrast to single
service programs, neighborhood centered multi-service projects address themselves to many of the roles of family members and can overcome the deficits of inadequate service
structures by instituting their own programs to meet the needs
of clients. The apparent effectiveness of single service casework projects resides in the novel and more efficient manner
of service delivery. Franklin County and Delaware program-
mers were quite successful in enabling experimental public
assistance workers to give more casework service to families
by reducing their caseload, and by concentrating efforts on
measures designed to improve the clients' economic status.

At the other end of the outcome continuum, what are
the factors that appear to be associated with the lack of positive results? From an elaborate post mortem which was held
examining the results of the Chemung County Study, [30] and the
interim project report of the CSS-DSS Study (the data have
not been fully analyzed at the time of this writing) we can
examine some of the underlying problems common to both.
Analysts of the Chemung County Study pointed out that it was
inappropriate to extend casework services to multi-problem
families when--to quote Helen Perlman--basic deficit needs
were not met. [31] In the Chemung County and the CSS-DSS
programs the relationship between experimental and control
action variables was confounded by the fact that the actual

treatment programs did not duplicate their designs.   In both
studies there was a serious lack of coordination between the
professional caseworkers and the public welfare authorities
with jurisdiction over the clients before the start of the research.   In Chemung County the reaching-out approach which
was to be used with demonstration cases was not implemented
until an advanced stage of the treatment phase. [32] The final
report on the CSS-DSS Study states that "in a strict sense
then, the collaborative program [between the Community Service Society and the Department of Social Services] as planned was not implemented. "[33]

The two problems associated with the Chemung
County and CSS-DSS studies, namely the failure to select
theoretically relevant types of intervention and the failure,
generally because of administrative difficulties, to implement
the conditions of the design in the intervention program, have
plagued many research projects.   They appeared to have been
more serious in these two studies than in the others, although
we are well aware of the fact that our post-hoc explanations
fall short of being a scientific interpretation of the causes of
failure.

The studies with positive as well as mixed outcome
offer an opportunity to look at the type of family functioning
which showed a direct relationship to the program of services.
Judging by the studies which identified components of change,
intervention in instrumental areas of social functioning appears to be more effective than in expressive areas.   This
was true for ADP, NIP, the Copenhagen Project, FLIP, and
to a large extent for the Midway Study, where most of the
changes under the heading "items related to children" and
"items related to adults" denoted instrumental behavior.   In
part, the gains in instrumental behavior by treatment group
families may be due to the deprived material status of most
of the study populations; they responded best to those services which met their most tangible and pressing needs.
Judging by the combined evidence including FLIP which served
a socially less disadvantaged population, it appears that advice, guidance, and support in such areas as child rearing,
health care, home-making, house hunting, etc. , had a sharper
impact upon family living than interpersonal counselling or
treatment of behavior problems.   The probable reason is
that, by and large, social work clients are most responsive
to help in areas where they can readily perceive and identify
problems and which carry less social stigma than problematic
intra- or interpersonal behavior.   The psychiatric tradition

of social work may mitigate against the recognition that the modification of problematic behavior is an area of weakness in professional helping. In fact, the analytically oriented agency may insist that ultimately it is only change in intra- and interpersonal function which counts. This happens to be a poorly researched area, but a position which is theoretically more defensible is that the avenues of change in behavior or social functioning may lie in instrumental or expressive-interpersonal areas, depending on such factors as age of family, social class, value system, state of well-being, types of problems experienced, level of unsatisfied needs,[34] and others. An insistence upon the primacy of interpersonal helping regardless of client situation or condition does little to advance professional practice.

Nearly all the experimental-control studies shared one theoretical shortcoming: they viewed social casework as a panacea for the problems of the target populations in spite of the fact that most of the people served were economically deprived. The public welfare related projects sought to meet the financial needs of their clients mainly within the limits of the rather inadequate public assistance provisions. FLIP and to a lesser extent the multi-service programs had a mandate for bringing clients into contact with community job training and job finding resources, but the quality of these resources along with the local employment situation set clear limits to the treatment objective of improving their economic status.

The effectiveness of casework was not only limited by lack of income or absence of steady employment; it was also influenced by the inability of poor clients to secure those material resources--decent housing, adequate medical services, a well balanced diet, good clothing, etc.--which are generally associated with an adequate income. The bulk of the intervention programs emphasized treatment techniques designed to change client attitudes and behavior. They were relatively powerless to alter the socio-economic environment. It is not argued here that client behavior had no need to change. Instead, we must question whether some types of behavior change are feasible in the absence of situational modifications and whether, in some instances, behavior change constitutes a poor substitute for environmental change. In short, there is need to ask whether the modest results of the outcome studies--testing either the effects of counselling or early intervention or more rational delivery systems--are not a function of the limitations of the intervention programs vis-à-vis the needs of the populations served.

This comparison of studies seriously challenges any attempt to assign such uniform labels as "successful" or "unsuccessful" to these research projects. Our categorization of results in terms of "major hypotheses disproven," "some of the major hypotheses supported," and "most of the major hypotheses supported" was equated in the discussion above with the designations "largely negative," "mixed," and "largely positive outcome." Whether one applied the label "success" to the latter group is a question of interpreting results relative to expectations, a term which is broader than the concept study hypotheses. Underlying practically every research report on these experimental-control studies is a sense of disappointment over the fact that the experiment did not yield the answer to the problem.

No profession, and certainly not social work, can be blamed for expressing itself optimistically regarding the power of its professional methods. It seems, however, that much of the infectious optimism of practitioners has been carried over to a large proportion of researchers, the present ones included, leading them to postulate hypotheses holding exaggerated views of social work capabilities. Significant improvements in total social functioning and the prevention of economic dependency not only strain the imagination of man but also make demands on many systems. Was the social worker, whether he acted as a counselor, therapist, advocate, giver of advice and information, referral agent, etc., confident that the above goals could be realized? If he was part of a multi-service project he was fortunate in having the support of a number of services, synchronized with his own, trying to meet a few client needs. If he sought to coordinate community services, the social worker was, of course, at their mercy and his effort could be no better than the service structure. Under the very best of circumstances professional intervention was able to bring to bear on the client only a limited number of the influences that would be needed if his overall social functioning were to be substantially altered. And so the pessimism expressed in the report on the findings is often the result of failure to countenance the lack of realism in the hypotheses.

A completely realistic formulation of hypotheses may actually be premature at this point for the simple reason that the profession has not taken a long, critical, and scientific look at its own performance. Not the least of the contributions of the Family Life Improvement Project and the other outcome studies may have been the provision of data for future, more realistic formulations of research and demonstration projects.

The discrepancies between some of the study hypotheses and the findings do not, however, detract from the basic worth of these studies as instruments for examing practice within a scientific framework.   Their execution and consequent responsible reporting have made it possible to examine the Family Life Improvement Project within a broader framework of related research.   And the collective evidence on results furnishes a modest platform for ending this report with some recommendations on service planning.

(1)   Since change in behavior and social situation is a function of many factors, there is need to rigorously define change targets and match programs, whether single or multi-faceted, with these targets.   No one type of program is likely to have a comprehensive impact, and yet many, if not most, competently administered services will probably show some measurable effect.   Change can come about in many ways: through problem focused counselling as in the Franklin County Project or through administrative reorganization as in the Midway Study.   Often, the most effective way of bringing about change may not be directly in the hands of the social work community but may require action by business and industry, labor unions, the housing authority, the educational system, the agencies of social control, and others.   Action by one or more of these may have a cumulative effect on the program of intervention offered by a social work agency.   That organization and its workers may have limited power to effect changes through professional channels in other systems whose deficiencies account for the client's problems.   The path to change may be outside the social work and social welfare orbit, in the realm of political and social action, and this might require activities by social workers in their roles as citizens rather than professionals.

(2)   Neighborhood or community focussed multi-service programs were shown to have achieved more positive results than projects with a limited intervention concern.   Multiple service programs, unlike those of a single service, do not rest their hope, as did FLIP, on inadequate service structures but seek through their own organizations to meet a variety of perceived needs.   The greater the deficiencies in the larger service structure the greater the need to mount a program that offers a variety of

resources and services. Multiple service endeavors are
naturally costly and, more likely than not, constitute but
a partial interim solution until the community, recognizing
its responsibility, mobilizes to meet the needs of its residents.

(3) The findings from an analysis of components of change
in FLIP and several of the other studies, point toward
the greater effectiveness of intervention in instrumental
rather than expressive and interpersonal areas of family
functioning, having implications for service planning. The
results demonstrated that the social worker, operating as
he did in areas identified with related professional fields
such as child care, public health, home economics, vocational counselling, etc. , did a reasonably creditable
job.   He found it necessary and appropriate to perform
many functions for which he had no special training or
scant in-service training at best.   If specialists from
these various fields would be incorporated, the effectiveness of these services would undoubtedly be enhanced.

A family-centered intervention program could bring together a multi-discipline service team, whose members
might receive special preparations for work with given
populations, such as the economically deprived or ethnic
minorities or unwed mothers, with service concentrated
mainly in the areas of their competence.   The Midway
Study demonstrated some of the real strengths of the team
approach in social work.   Trained and/or experienced
social workers might serve as team leaders or supervisors, and take it upon themselves to deal with situations
involving problems in behavior or interpersonal relationships.   A careful assessment of a family's dominant need
or problem may lead to the assignment of a specialist as
the main worker, who could, with the aid of in-service
training and supervision, address himself to other problems that need to be dealt with or call in additional specialists, acting as the coordinator of their services.

The experiences of most of the action research projects
indicate that persons with undergraduate training, operating under professional supervision, can perform quite
effectively, especially as members of a team.   A multi-
service mode of operation may not, however, reach its
optimum level of effectiveness until training for these
roles has been incorporated into professional education
and become available to those ready to serve on such
teams.

(4) The preventive approach, a key issue in the Family Life
    Improvement Project, has received some support from
    the results of this action-research endeavor, which showed
    that early intervention makes a measurable difference in
    a few specified areas. Not showing statistically signifi-
    cant change in all areas of family functioning, FLIP re-
    vealed the same weaknesses as most of the other outcome
    studies discussed in this chapter. Intervention, ameliora-
    tive or preventive, did not and could not possibly affect
    all those tasks and roles which called for improvement.
    On the other hand, there is ample evidence that preven-
    tive intervention is a realistic endeavor, for FLIP data
    showed that families functioning relatively adequately at
    the start of the Project gained as much from the program
    as families manifesting various kinds of malfunctioning.
    Whether the ounce of prevention which improved the role
    and task performances of treatment group families rela-
    tive to the control group was indeed worth a pound of
    cure can only be answered by long term follow-up re-
    search.

The architects of prevention programs face essentially
the same issues as the planners of ameliorative services--
although perhaps on an even larger scale--because preventive measures have to be applied in a more universal manner. Genuine prevention has to come to grips with all the
family roles which are potentially in jeopardy, whether
these be the roles of mother, homemaker, husband, ten-
ant of a dwelling unit, money manager, or wage earner.
Prevention in the broadest sense means providing as many
early supports as the family will need for later development. The preventive approach to family malfunctioning
can be strengthened by family planning, child rearing
guidance, family life education, marriage counselling, and
related services, but its foundation is based on economic
and social security. Unfortunately, these are the two
factors which many Americans, especially those in lower-
status and minority groups, are lacking.

While the Family Life Improvement Project pointed out
some of the limits of intervention based largely on interpersonal helping, it also demonstrated quite clearly the
readiness of young families to use whatever measures
were offered on their behalf. Extended voluntary participation of the vast bulk of those originally recruited for
the Project[35] testifies to the fact that young urban families are willing to invest themselves in improving the

quality of their lives. This knowledge has implications for social planning in a society which has enthroned the myth of self-reliance at the expense of building institutions for serving people.

Notes

1. The very well designed and executed study by Reid and Shyne, Brief and Extended Casework, was ruled out because it compared two alternative methods of casework, neither of which could be said to constitute a condition of no service or minimal service. See William J. Reid and Ann W. Shyne, Brief and Extended Casework, New York: Columbia University Press, 1969.

2. Joseph Lagey and Beverly Ayres, Community Treatment Programs for Multi-Problem Families, Vancouver, B. C. : Community Chest and Councils of the Greater Vancouver Area, December 1962, p. 2.

3. Edward A. Suchman, Evaluative Research, New York: Russell Sage Foundation, 1967. See especially Chapters VI, VII, and IX.

4. Geismar and Krisberg, The Forgotten Neighborhood, op. cit.

5. Bell and Wilder, op. cit.

6. Brown, op. cit. , p. 122.

7. Wilson, loc. cit.

8. Bell and Wilder, op. cit.

9. Bell and Wilder, op. cit. , p. 53.

10. Geismar and Krisberg, The Forgotten Neighborhood.

11. Of six agencies which started the project together, only one remained to the end. Ibid. , pp. 278-293.

12. Brown, op. cit.

13. Kühl, op. cit.

14. Ibid., p. 193.

15. Ibid., p. 197.

16. Ibid., p. 192.

17. Behling, op. cit.

18. Mullen et al., op. cit.

19. Ibid., p. 1.

20. Schwartz and Sample, loc. cit.

21. For instance, Plan A introduced a new but relatively simple case classification plan. Ibid., p. 122.

22. Nearly half the cases served were individual clients. Other aspects covered by the study were the effects of the experiment upon staff attitude and performance.

23. The investigators chose the 10% rather than the 5% level of significance.

24. Wilson, loc. cit., and Community Service Council of Delaware, op. cit.

25. Neither the article nor the full project report gave information on the number of interviews conducted.

26. These two studies could not be termed as having produced entirely negative results, for some of the findings showed quite consistent differences in the direction hypothesized, although they fell short of statistical significance.

27. Behling, op. cit., p. 3.

28. Geismar and Krisberg, The Forgotten Neighborhood, op. cit., pp. 354-369.

29. See L. L. Geismar and Beverly Ayres, Patterns of Change in Problem Families, St. Paul, Minn. : Family Centered Project, 1959, p. 12.

30. Brown, op. cit., pp. 32-106.

31. Ibid., p. 65.

32. Ibid., p. 114.

33. Mullen et al., op. cit., p. 205.

34. Maslow reasons that when lower level needs (physiological and security needs) dominate the organism, they must be satisfied before those of a higher level, such as the need for belonging and self-esteem, can be dealt with. It can be argued that for most of the study populations instrumental problems and needs dominated over expressive ones. This fact could account for their more positive movement in areas of instrumental functioning. See A. H. Maslow, "A Theory of Human Motivation," Psychological Review, Vol. 50, No. 4, 1943, pp. 370-396.

35. As shown in Chapter 7, only 61 treatment group families out of the original 272 (or, 22.4%) refused to continue treatment to the end.

APPENDICES

APPENDIX A. Comparison of Experimental and Control
Families on Selected Variables[a]

Table A1. Ethnicity of Families Who Continued to End of Study by Experimental and Control Groups

Race	Treatment Group (N=177) %	Control Group (N=175) %
Negro	62.7	65.7
White	31.1	29.7
Puerto Rican	6.2	4.6
	100.0	100.0

Table A2. Marital Status of Families Who Continued to End of Study by Experimental and Control Groups

Marital Status	Treatment Group (N=177) %	Control Group (N=175) %
Married	62.2	66.9
Out-of-Wedlock	36.7	31.4
Separated, Widowed, Divorced	1.1	1.7
	100.0	100.0

Table A3. Social Class of Families Who Continued to End of Study by Experimental and Control Groups

Social Class	Treatmentb Group (N=175) %	Control Group (N=175) %
I to IV	14.3	17.1
V	42.3	42.3
VI	43.4	40.6
	100.0	100.0

Table A4. Beginning Scores by Treatment and Control Groups

Beginning Total Family Functioning Scores	Treatment Group (N=177) %	Control Group (N=175) %
Most Adequate (53-56)	34.5	38.8
Moderately Adequate (47-52)	33.9	36.6
Least Adequate (46 & below)	31.6	24.6
	100.0	100.0

a. The computation of the chi square for the four tables above revealed a p-level that was statistically not significant.

b. For two families in the treatment group information needed to identify social class was missing.

APPENDIX B

Summary of Sample Validation Study*

The failure to find 49% of the potentially eligible families (585 out of 1,198) randomly selected for inclusion in the
study led the research staff to engage in an evaluation of the
representativeness of the study sample. This investigation
took the form of a comparison of a 10% randomly selected
sample of families who were contacted and interviewed at the
outset of the study with a 10% random sample of families who
were not found initially.

The two sub-samples were compared on readily available demographic characteristics and on the major dependent
variable of family functioning.

Comparing respondents and non-respondents constituting
a sample of available demographic factors is a common method of assessing sample bias in the social sciences. It is
based on the assumption that where there is a strong correlation between demographic factors and the dependent variable,
the extent to which respondents and non-respondents in the
sample are alike on the dependent variable can be inferred
from the extent to which they show equivalence on the demographic characteristics.

After extensive tracking efforts we succeeded in locating and interviewing 77% of the originally missing families
in the sub-sample. Thus, the sample bias study is based on
59 families from the group of Project participants and 40
families from the group which could not originally be found.

We found that the two sub-samples did not differ significantly on a variety of demographic factors but did differ
significantly on the major dependent variable of family functioning. The families which could not be located initially
were found to function more poorly than families who were
interviewed at the outset (chi square = 5.90, 1 d.f., p < .02).

196

The results of the study suggest that the comparison of respondents and non-respondents on demographic data alone may produce erroneous conclusions about sample representativeness relative to the dependent variable.

In attempting to answer the question of representativeness of the FLIP sample, we carried out some calculations based on the assumption that the levels of social functioning of initially interviewed and originally missing cases both differ from the true universe of cases, each representing extremes in accessibility and correlated social functioning. While the true universe is not actually known, an approximation can be obtained by estimating the combined distribution on the social functioning dimension by means of combining the weighted (for their respective N's) scores for these two groups. Comparing the estimated universe to the study sample, it was thought, will give some idea about sample representativeness. When the combined scores (assumed to approximate the true universe) are compared with the scores of the original Project participants, differences are still observed but they do not reach statistical significance (chi square = 5.59, 2 d.f., p < .10).

The question still remains as to what the comparison would yield had it been possible to interview the 23% of the sub-sample of originally missing families who still could not be found. Insofar as the data show that less adequate functioning is associated with inability to be located, we might expect these 23% to be more problematic than the 77% eventually found and interviewed.

In short, even though the analysis failed to produce precise data as to the extent to which the sample deviated from the universe, the converging evidence strongly points to an overrepresentation of relatively well functioning families and an underrepresentation of poorly functioning families in the study sample. Nonetheless, failure to prove sample representativeness relative to universe was not viewed as a problem in outcome measurement since we succeeded, as is shown elsewhere in this report (Chapter 6 and Appendix A), to carry out the study with comparable experimental and control groups.

---

*This is a brief summary of a fuller report by Bruce W. Lagay appearing in the paper entitled "Finding Lost Respondents: A Field Procedure for Locating Inaccessible Respondents When Assessing Dependent Variable Bias in an Incompletely Constituted Random Sample," Rutgers Grad. School of Social Work (1968 (Mimeo).

See also Bruce W. Lagay, "Assessing Bias: A Comparison of Two Methods," The Public Opinion Quarterly, Vol. 33, No. 4, Winter 1969/70, pp. 615-618.

APPENDIX C.   Comparison of Change Scores in Sub-Groups of
Control Group Families[a]

Category	Families Seen Once a Year (N=88)[b] %			Families Seen Two-Three Times a Year (N=49)[b] %			Families Seen Before-After (N=38)[b] %		
	Positive Movement	No Change	Negative Movement	Positive Movement	No Change	Negative Movement	Positive Movement	No Change	Negative Movement
Family Relationships & Unity	28.4	44.3	27.3	22.4	53.1	24.5	18.4	55.3	26.3
Individual Behavior & Adjustment	28.4	43.2	28.4	30.6	46.9	22.5	13.2	60.5	26.3
Care & Training of Children	14.8	34.1	51.1	8.2	42.8	49.0	18.4	39.5	42.1
Social Activities	25.0	51.1	23.9	22.4	63.3	14.3	21.1	57.8	21.1

Economic Practices	26.1	44.4	29.5	16.3	36.7	47.0	28.9	55.3	15.8
Home & Household Practices	26.1	45.5	28.4	40.9	36.7	22.4	23.7	47.4	28.9
Health Conditions & Practices	26.1	38.7	35.2	32.7	28.6	38.7	15.8	57.9	26.3
Use of Community Resources	25.0	65.9	9.1	16.3	75.5	8.2	15.8	68.4	15.8
Total Score	37.5	14.8	47.7	36.7	12.2	51.1	47.3	13.2	39.5

a. Differences among the 3 sub-groups with respect to movement in 7 categories and total score were found not to be statistically significant. The exception was the category Economic Practices, which was found significant at less than the .05 level.

b. The N's in the above table vary slightly from the attrition rate reported in Chapter 2 because of transfer of cases among frequency of contact categories.

APPENDIX D. Matrix of Pearsonian Correlations Among Main Category Family Functioning Scores for Treatment and Control Families at Start of Project

	Indiv. Behavior	Care & Trng. of Children	Social Activities	Econ. Practices	Household Practices	Health Con. & Practices	Use of Community Resources	Total Scores*
Family Relationship	.807	.596	.651	.548	.386	.436	.441	.705
Individual Behavior		.664	.716	.635	.517	.513	.546	.779
Care/Training of Children			.513	.530	.520	.615	.587	.666
Soc. Activities				.511	.378	.411	.443	.678
Econ. Practices					.558	.579	.522	.703
Home/Household Practices						.568	.470	.686
Health Condit. & Practices							.659	.624
Community Resources Use								.578

For statistical significance at the .001 level correlation coefficient must be at least .32.

*Total scores for purposes of machine analysis were divided into four score groupings.

APPENDIX E. Diverse Characteristics of Treatment
Group Compared at the Beginning and End of Project

TABLE E1.
Comparison of Demographic Characteristics
of Population Served and Original Treatment Group

Demographic Characteristics	Population Served N=177[a]	Original Treatment Group N=272[b]
Race, Ethnicity, and Nativity	Percent	Percent
Negro	62	59
White (native born, non-Spanish speaking)	27	33
Spanish speaking Latins[c]	8	6
Others[d]	3	3
Total	100	100
Social Class[e]		
Class I[f] and II	1	2
Class III	6	7
Class IV	7	9
Class V	42	42
Class VI	44	40
Total	100	100
Marital Status		
Married	64	68
Unmarried	36	32
Total	100	100

a. Minor discrepancies between these data and the data in Appendix A are due to variations in certain of the breakdowns used.
b. Because of attrition in this group, incomplete data exists on all 272 families and N's for selected demographic characteristics vary as follows: Race, Ethnicity, and Nativity, N=264; Social Class, N=257; Marital Status, N=262.
c. One Portugese speaking family from Brazil included here.
d. Immigrants from outside the hemisphere.
e. Stratification based on the William Wells' adaptation of the Hollingshead two factor Index of Social Position.
f. One family each in Classes I and II in the Population Served and two families each in Classes I and II in the Original Treatment Group.

TABLE E2

Comparison of Beginning Family
Functioning Scores of Population
Served and Original Treatment Group

Beginning Family Functioning Scores[a]	% of Families Served (N=177)	Percentage of Original Treatment Group (N=263[b])
63-59	36	24
58-54	29	31
53-49	15	20
48-44	12	15
43 and below	8	10
	100	100

a. Scores are based on nine, rather than eight, areas of family functioning. The ninth area is Relationship to FLIP Worker.
b. Nine cases in the original treatment group did not have complete enough information to permit the computation of beginning family functioning scores.

APPENDIXES F & G

FAMILY LIFE IMPROVEMENT PROJECT
WEEKLY TREATMENT LOG

Client.............................. FLIP #......... Worker............................. Week of.........

Col. #	I	II	
Date			
Profile Cat. and Sub-cat.			
Spec. Subj.			
Person(s)			
Place and Mode of Contact			
Initiated by			
Worker Activity			
Client Activity and Attitude			
(Activity of Others)			

Time Summary: Time with Client...................... Administrative Time ....

Time with Collaterals .... Supervision and/or Consultation Time ....

APPENDIX F

III	IV	V

Change of Status Entry:

APPENDIX G

FAMILY LIFE IMPROVEMENT PROJECT

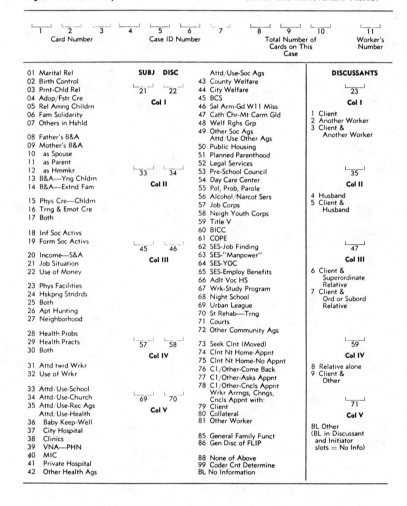

1	2	3	4	5	6	7	8	9	10	11
Card Number				Case ID Number			Total Number of Cards on This Case			Worker's Number

01 Marital Rel	**SUBJ** **DISC**	Attd/Use-Soc Ags		**DISCUSSANTS**
02 Birth Control		43 County Welfare		
03 Prnt-Chld Rel	21 22	44 City Welfare		23
04 Adop/Fstr Cre	**Col I**	45 BCS		**Col I**
05 Rel Amng Childrn		46 Sal Arm-Gd W11 Miss		
06 Fam Solidarity		47 Cath Chr-Mt Carm Gld		1 Client
07 Others in Hshld		48 Welf Rghs Grp		2 Another Worker
		49 Other Soc Ags		3 Client &
08 Father's B&A		Attd/Use Other Ags		Another Worker
09 Mother's B&A		50 Public Housing		
10 as Spouse		51 Planned Parenthood		
11 as Parent		52 Legal Services		
12 as Hmmkr	33 34	53 Pre-School Council		35
13 B&A—Yng Chldrn	**Col II**	54 Day Care Center		**Col II**
14 B&A—Extnd Fam		55 Pol, Prob, Parole		
15 Phys Cre—Chldrn		56 Alcohol/Narcot Sers		4 Husband
16 Trng & Emot Cre		57 Job Corps		5 Client &
17 Both		58 Neigh Youth Corps		Husband
		59 Title V		
18 Inf Soc Activs		60 BICC		
19 Form Soc Activs	45 46	61 COPE		47
		62 SES-Job Finding		
20 Income—S&A	**Col III**	63 SES-"Manpower"		**Col III**
21 Job Situation		64 SES-YOC		
22 Use of Money		65 SES-Employ Benefits		6 Client &
		66 Adlt Voc HS		Superordinate
23 Phys Facilities		67 Wrk-Study Program		Relative
24 Hskpng Stndrds		68 Night School		7 Client &
25 Both		69 Urban League		Ord or Subord
26 Apt Hunting		70 St Rehab—Trng		Relative
27 Neighborhood		71 Courts		
		72 Other Community Ags		
28 Health Probs				
29 Health Practs	57 58	73 Seek Clnt (Moved)		59
30 Both	**Col IV**	74 Clnt Nt Home-Appnt		**Col IV**
		75 Clnt Nt Home-No Appnt		
31 Attd twrd Wrkr		76 Cl/Other-Come Back		8 Relative alone
32 Use of Wrkr		77 Cl/Other-Asks Appnt		9 Client &
		78 Cl/Other-Cncls Appnt		Other
33 Attd/Use-School		Wrkr Arrngs, Chngs,		
34 Attd/Use-Church	69 70	Cncls Appnt with:		
35 Attd/Use-Rec Ags	**Col V**	79 Client		71
Attd/Use-Health		80 Collateral		**Col V**
36 Baby Keep-Well		81 Other Worker		
37 City Hospital				
38 Clinics		85 General Family Funct		BL Other
39 VNA—PHN		86 Gen Disc of FLIP		(BL in Discussant
40 MIC				and Initiator
41 Private Hospital		88 None of Above		slots = No Info)
42 Other Health Ags		99 Coder Cnt Determine		
		BL No Information		

APPENDIX G

12	13		14	15	16		17	18	19		20
Wk of Rx for This Case				FLIP Wk of Rx			C1/Col	Ad Time Analysis	Sup		Place & Mode of Contact

INITIATOR		TIME ANALYSIS Cols 17-18-19	PLACE & MODE OF CONTACT	WORKER—CLIENT			
	24	1 15 mins or—	1 Home Visit	25	26	27	28
	Col I	2 ½ hr	2 Phone	**Col I** Worker			
1 Client		3 1 hr	3 Comm Res				
2 Worker		4 1½ hrs	4 HV + P	29	30	31	32
		5 2 hrs	5 HV + CR	**Client**			
		6 2½ hrs	6 P + CR				
		7 3 hrs	7 HV + P + CR				
		8 3½ hrs	8 Office				
		9 3½ hrs +	9 Other				
	36	BL No Info	BL No Info	37	38	39	40
	Col II			**Col II** Worker			
3 Other re Client		**WORKER—CLIENT ACTIVITY**					
4 Other re Self			Ask Off Giv Res	41	42	43	44
		Information	11 21 31 41	**Client**			
		Support	12 22 32				
		Advice & Guid	13 23 33 43				
	48	Pract Help	14 24 34 44	49	50	51	52
	Col III	Analysis	15 25 35	**Col III** Worker			
5 Client re Other							
6 Other Worker re Clnt or FLIP		Sets Task	16 26 36 46	53	54	55	56
7 Other Worker re Self		Reviews Task	17 27 37 47	**Client**			
		Coords-Other Wrkr	18 28 48				
		Intercedes- "	19 29 49				
		Help-General	51 52				
		Listens	61	61	62	63	64
	60	+ Affect	71	**Col IV** Worker			
	Col IV	— Affect	81				
8 Other re Others		Accept	72	65	66	67	68
		Rejects	82	**Client**			
		C1 no qual fr prg	91				
	72	C1 accept fr prg	92				
	Col V	C1 enter prg	93	73	74	75	76
9 Coder Cnt Deter		C1 gets + $	94	**Col V** Worker			
BL No Information		C1 gets — $	95				
		C1 reject fr prg	96	77	78	79	80
		C1 rec FLIP $	97	**Client**			
		Only one action	98				
		Coder Cant Determine	99				
		No Information	BL				

APPENDIX H. Treatment and Control Groups Compared on Diverse Socio-Economic Indices of Change

	Treatment Group (%)			Control Group (%)		
	Begin.	End	Difference Between Beginning And End	Begin.	End	Difference Between Beginning And End
Fully Self-Supporting						
Unmarried Parents	9.5	30.2	20.7	5.5	25.5	20.0
Married Parents	88.2	90.9	2.7	92.3	91.5	-.8
Remaining Self-Supporting		94.2		94.6		
Not Self-Supporting at start; self-supporting at end.		30.1			25.4	
Income below $4,000	42.2	30.7	-11.5	30.4	23.1	-7.3
Mean No. Children:						
Unmarried Parents		1.79				2.04
Married Parents		1.88				1.96
Unwed mothers married by end		11.3			18.2	
Married parents divorced or separated by end		10.2			8.5	

	Col 1	Col 2	Col 3	Col 4	Col 5	Col 6
Families with member known to Parole/Probation Services	6.3	8.6	2.3	3.6	4.3	.7
Families with member in penal/correctional institution	5.6	7.3	1.7	3.4	4.0	.6
Families who say they use public employment agency	12.1	16.6	4.5	7.4	9.7	2.3
Families who say they use OEO	11.3	21.0	9.7	1.7	12.1	10.4
Families who say they use recreational facilities	5.1	12.0	6.9	2.9	5.9	3.0
Families who say they use public parks, playgrounds	34.3	49.1	14.8	41.1	68.5	27.4
Mothers who say they participate in church activities	8.0	7.4	-.6	15.1	19.4	4.3
Mothers who belong to social/recreational group	6.3	12.6	6.3	7.0	11.2	4.2
Mothers who use health services (public)	58.5	53.7	-4.8	62.1	52.7	-9.4
Medical resources family uses: Public facilities only	21.5	18.1	-3.4	23.6	16.1	-7.5
Private facilities only	40.7	46.9	6.2	40.2	48.9	8.7
Both	37.9	35.0	-2.9	36.2	35.1	-1.1

APPENDIX I.

Questionnaire for Client's Self-Evaluation of Family Functioning

As part of our study of families who have been part of the Family
Life Improvement Project, we would like to find out how you think
things have changed for you and your family between the time when
we first came to see you and the present. Please indicate in every
area by a circle whether a change occurred in your situation, and
if so, how much of a change. If you don't know the answer to the
question, or if it is not relevant, circle where appropriate.

The Situation Now Is:

	(1) Much Worse	(2) Slightly Worse	(3) No Change	(4) Slightly Better	(5) Much Better	(0) Don't Know	Not Rele- vant
1. How do you and your husband get along generally? (10)	W	w	Nc	b	B	?	Nr
2. Has there been any change in how you and your husband put up with each other's moods? (11)	W	w	Nc	b	B	?	Nr

#	Question	W	w	Nc	b	B	?	Nr
3. (12)	Any changes in how you and your husband discuss problems and share feelings?	W	w	Nc	b	B	?	Nr
4. (13)	Any change in how you get along sexually?	W	w	Nc	b	B	?	Nr
5. (14)	Any change in the way you and your husband feel about each other's leisure time activities?	W	w	Nc	b	B	?	Nr
6. (15)	How do you and your husband get along with your children?	W	w	Nc	b	B	?	Nr
7. (16)	Has there been a change in how you feel about your children?	W	w	Nc	b	B	?	Nr
8. (17)	How do the children in your home get along with each other?	W	w	Nc	b	B	?	Nr
9. (18)	Has there been any change in how you and your husband plan for the future?	W	w	Nc	b	B	?	Nr

	(1) Much Worse	(2) Slightly Worse	(3) No Change	(4) Slightly Better	(5) Much Better	(0) Don't Know	Not Relevant
10. (19) Any change in how you, as a family, do things together?	W	w	Nc	b	B	?	Nr
11. (20) Any change in how, you as a family, "pull together" in times of trouble?	W	w	Nc	b	B	?	Nr
12. (21) If someone other than your husband, children, or your parents live with you, has there been any change in how all of you have been getting along together?	W	w	Nc	b	B	?	Nr
13. (22) Has there been any change in how you feel about yourself?	W	w	Nc	b	B	?	Nr

Question	W	w	Nc	b	B	?	Nr
14. Do you feel that the way you dress and general appearance has changed since we first saw you? (23)	W	w	Nc	b	B	?	Nr
15. Has there been any change in how you get along with people in general? (24)	W	w	Nc	b	B	?	Nr
16. Do you think there has been any change in how your husband (wife) feels about himself and gets along with people in general? (25)	W	w	Nc	b	B	?	Nr
17. Has there been any change in the condition and amount of your children's clothing? (26)	W	w	Nc	b	B	?	Nr
18. Any change in how you feed and generally take care of your children? (27)	W	w	Nc	b	B	?	Nr

	(1) Much Worse	(2) Slightly Worse	(3) No Change	(4) Slightly Better	(5) Much Better	(0) Don't Know	Not Relevant
19. Any change in how you and your husband agree on disciplining the children? (28)	W	w	Nc	b	B	?	Nr
20. Any change in the way you actually discipline the children? (29)	W	w	Nc	b	B	?	Nr
21. Has there been a change in how you get along with your family and your husband's (wife's) family? (30)	W	w	Nc	b	B	?	Nr
22. Has anything changed in how you get along with your neighbors? (31)	W	w	Nc	b	B	?	Nr
23. Any change in satisfaction with the way you spend your free time? (32)	W	w	Nc	b	B	?	Nr
24. Has there been any change in the way you and your							

	W	w	Nc	b	B	?	Nr
husband (wife) participate in clubs, unions and other (33) organizations?	W	w	Nc	b	B	?	Nr
25. Any change in how you or your husband feel about belonging to clubs and other (34) organizations?	W	w	Nc	b	B	?	Nr
26. Since services started what changes have there been in (35) your actual cash income?	W	w	Nc	b	B	?	Nr
27. How satisfied are you with your present income as compared to the way you felt about your income when services (36) started?	W	w	Nc	b	B	?	Nr
28. How does your present income, compared to previous income, meet your actual (37) needs?	W	w	Nc	b	B	?	Nr
29. If you, or your husband are employed has there been (38) a change in job satisfaction?	W	w	Nc	b	B	?	Nr

	(1) Much Worse	(2) Slightly Worse	(3) No Change	(4) Slightly Better	(5) Much Better	(0) Don't Know	Not Relevant
30. Is that job more suited to your or your husband's abilities than before? (39)	W	w	Nc	b	B	?	Nr
31. Has there been a change in how you and your husband (wife) agree on how money ought to be spent? (40)	W	w	Nc	b	B	?	Nr
32. If you have any debts is there any change in how you are able to meet payment on these debts? (41)	W	w	Nc	b	B	?	Nr
33. What kind of money managers or budgeters are you now as compared to then? (42)	W	w	Nc	b	B	?	Nr
34. Any change in the kind of apartment or house which you now occupy? (43)	W	w	Nc	b	B	?	Nr
35. Is the neighborhood you live in better or worse now? (44)	W	w	Nc	b	B	?	Nr

		W	w	Nc	b	B	?	Nr
36.	Has there been a change in the quantity or quality of your household furniture and furnishings? (45)	W	w	Nc	b	B	?	Nr
37.	Has there been a change in your (or your wife's) housekeeping habits? (46)	W	w	Nc	b	B	?	Nr
38.	Have you changed in the way you (or your wife) serve and plan meals? (47)	W	w	Nc	b	B	?	Nr
39.	Has there been a change in the ease with which you (or your wife) perform your household chores? (48)	W	w	Nc	b	B	?	Nr
40.	How is your health and that of members of your immediate family now as compared to the time services began? (49)	W	w	Nc	b	B	?	Nr
41.	Have there been changes in the way you take care of your and your family's health needs? (50)	W	w	Nc	b	B	?	Nr

	(1) Much Worse	(2) Slightly Worse	(3) No Change	(4) Slightly Better	(5) Much Better	(0) Don't Know	Not Relevant
42. Any change in the manner in which you get medical and dental check-ups or keep appointments? (51)	W	w	Nc	b	B	?	Nr
43. Has there been a change in how you feel about schools and education for your children? (52)	W	w	Nc	b	B	?	Nr
44. Has there been any change in your church or synagogue-going habits? (53)	W	w	Nc	b	B	?	Nr
45. Are there any changes in the way you use health resources, such as clinics, private doctors, hospitals? (54)	W	w	Nc	b	B	?	Nr
46. How do you now use social agencies as compared to when services started? (55)	W	w	Nc	b	B	?	Nr
47. Has there been a change in how you use recreational agencies? (56)	W	w	Nc	b	B	?	Nr

48. Have your feelings toward
and opinion about, community
resources in general changed?

(57)   W   w   Nc   b   B   ?   Nr

49. Do you believe your knowledge
about community resources in
general has changed?

(58)   W   w   Nc   b   B   ?   Nr

50. How do you feel things have changed for you as a result of our coming to see you?

(59) _____

(60) _____

(61) _____

(62) _____

(63) _____

(64) _____

(65) _____

(66) _____

(67) _____

APPENDIX J

A Comparison of Three Approaches
to Assessing Outcome

In the latter portion of Chapter 8, we presented the results obtained from questioning the client about the changes she believed to have taken place since she began participating in the Family Life Improvement Project. These data were part of a larger attempt to study the relationships among various modes of assessing movement, including the client's self-evaluation. In this section we present the results of this broader investigation.

In Chapter 8 three studies concerned with the correspondence between practitioner and client assessment of outcome were cited[1] but discussed only briefly because their focus was more on consensus between the two sources of judgment than on client self-evaluation per se. Further attention will be given here to the findings of the three studies for they have relevance to the present analysis.

In the study by Elizabeth Most a high degree of correspondence between client's self-evaluation and worker's judgment of movement was found. But contrary to the findings of that study, Sacks, Bradley, and Beck found that the degree of client-worker consensus in case-by-case comparison was fairly low when compared to a global assessment of change (agreement between worker and client was found in slightly over half the cases). It was found to be lower still when specific dimensions of functioning were considered. According to the authors, this is consistent with most other studies employing an interview technique which elicits the client's own evaluation of movement. They found that workers tended to be more conservative in their judgments than their clients and less likely to perceive positive change. Worker-client agreement was greatest in those areas in which there was most contact with clients and, consequently, access to the greatest amount of information. Correspondingly, in those areas in which contact was most limited, information was likely to be minimal; as a result the worker and client were more apt to disagree about the direction of change. Another finding reported by these researchers was that workers varied considerably in the extent to which they agreed with clients, suggesting to the authors that there were considerable differences in the sensitivity of the workers.

In the study carried out by John Crane and associates, the findings differed from those of the Sack's study, for more conservatism was found on the part of clients; the workers were the ones who tended to see more positive change. The following areas of functioning were identified as those in which the discrepancy between worker and client was greatest: marital, parent-child, and sibling relationships and the informal social relationships between the family and friends or relatives.

The foregoing studies will enable us to view our own effort within the context of previous endeavors using client evaluation on the judgment of outcome. Comparisons between our own findings and those discussed above will be made at the end of this analysis. First, we will compare the responses of clients and workers to the structured questionnaire on the client's movement [discussed in Chapter 8; a copy is shown in Appendix I]. Then we will analyze the relationship between change measured by the structured questionnaire and movement determined by the Profile ratings. Subsequently, we will explore the factors associated with agreement between worker and client, and finally, examine worker differences in rates of agreement with clients.

As we have already indicated, a procedure was developed to score the client assessment of movement (see note 7, Chapter 8). In addition, the present analysis necessitated the development of the following indices:

a) A score for each area of family functioning and for overall functioning as well, indicative of the worker's assessment of change according to the structured instrument. [2]

b) An index[3] for each area of functioning and for overall functioning denoting the nature and extent of agreement between the client and the worker. This was employed both for obtaining an overall picture of the degree of agreement and for correlating it with other factors.

Here are the findings based on 157 treatment families who responded to the structured instrument and their workers. [3]

Agreement between worker and client based on responses to structured questionnaire

These findings tend to be more in line with Most's[4] work than with Sack's,[5] for the data show a high degree of agreement between client and worker. When we examined this agreement on overall functioning, we found that 86% of the client-worker pairs agreed on the direction of change and only 14% of the pairs disagreed. Of the former group, most or 70.1% agreed that positive change had occurred, a minority or 15.9% agreed that no change had resulted, and none of the client-worker pairs concurred that the situation had become worse. As to the 14% of the client-worker pairs exhibiting disagreement on movement, the proportion of pairs in which the client was more positive than the worker slightly exceeded the proportion in which the reverse was true. (The percentages were 8.3 and 5.7, respectively.) These findings fail to support the results of either Sack's study or Crane's concerning the relative conservatism of workers' judgment compared to that of clients.

Turning to degree of agreement in the main categories of family functioning, we find a pattern similar to that described above. Depending on the area, the percentage of client-worker pairs in which there was consensus on direction of change ranged from a low of 64.5% (Social Activities) to a high of 84.6% (Economic Practices and Conditions). (The rank order of all main categories of functioning is shown below in Table J.1.) The modal pattern for all but two categories was for pairs to agree that movement had been positive. The exceptions were Health Conditions and Practices in which the modal pattern was for pairs to agree on no change and Social Activities in which two modal patterns were noted--agreement on no change and agreement on positive change. No more than 5% of the pairs in any of the eight areas agreed that their functioning had deteriorated. Examining the discrepancies between worker and client, we find that the percentage of pairs who disagreed about the direction of change ranged from 15.4% to 45.4%, the mean percent being equal to 25.7. In all areas but one, Economic Practices, the percentage of pairs in which the client was more positive when disagreement occurred slightly exceeded the percentage of pairs in which the worker was more positive.

Although highly tentative, the finding that agreement is lowest in the area of Social Activities and highest in the area of Economic Practices and Conditions offers limited evidence in support of the point made by Sacks et al.[6]--

that agreement is lowest in those areas in which the worker has least access to information. In this study considerable emphasis was given to problems related to functioning in the Economic area. At the same time, because of numerous more pressing problems and needs, the area of Social Activities was one to which the worker might have devoted slightly less attention, and consequently have been more poorly informed.

Table J.1. Areas of Functioning Ranked
by Percent of Client-Worker Pairs Who
Agreed on Direction of Changes

Area of Functioning	% of Pairs Agreeing
Economic Conditions and Practices	84.6
Individual Behavior and Adjustment	81.8
Use of Community Resources	74.3
Household Conditions and Practices	73.1
Care and Training of Children	73.0
Family Relationships and Unity	72.7
Health Conditions and Practices	70.5
Social Activities	64.5

Relationship between change as determined by the structured
instrument and change as measured by the Profile ratings

The relationships between the two measures of change, examined separately for worker and for client, revealed similar patterns. [7] For both the worker and the client, a positive relationship of moderate strength was observed between assessment of overall change as determined by the structured instrument and that measured by the Profile ratings. Gammas equal to +.347 for the worker and +.329 for the client were obtained. An examination of the degree of correspondence between the two measures of movement in the main categories of functioning for both worker and client showed that, in all but one area each, the relationships were positive but tended to be weaker than for overall functioning. Correspondence between the worker's assessment of the client's movement as measured by the Profile was least in the area of Social Activities, the only category in which a negative gamma was found (-.088), and greatest in the Use of Community Resources (gamma = +.313). Discrepancies between the client's evaluation of movement and movement assessed by Profile ratings were greatest in the category Child Care and Training, the sole area in which the relationship was negative (-.031), and least in the category Health Conditions and Practices (gamma = +.337).

Failure to find positive relationships of considerable strength between the two ways of assessing change may be attributed to both inaccuracies and differences in the judgment of worker, client, and/or rater, and factors related to the characteristics of the two instruments. No attempt will be made to assess the relative contribution of each of the two factors to the relatively low level of correspondence between the two kinds of measures. The reader's attention is called to the fact that fairly substantial changes would have had to occur for a rating of a Profile to be lowered or raised, whereas relatively minor alterations in the functioning of the family might have resulted in the client or worker responding "better" or "worse", as the case may be. Furthermore, it was not possible, using the Profile mode of measurement, for a client rated as adequate throughout the study to show positive movement, yet adequacy is not equated to functioning which is completely problem-free. Thus, changes may have occurred which while not large enough to make a coder modify his rating, may have produced a response to the structured instrument of "better" or "worse", as the case may be, from the worker or client. To some extent this is substantiated by the finding that a considerable proportion (for many areas this is a modal pattern) of those who indicate that things had changed for the better showed "no movement" according to the Profile rating.

Let us return to the findings pertaining to the relationship between movement based on the Profile and the client's self-evaluation. The evidence does not support the interpretation offered previously, namely, that correspondence between professional and client judgment depends on amount of information. Child Care and Training, the area in which the greatest discrepancy between client and Profile ratings occurred, was an area given considerable emphasis by the FLIP worker, and the Profiles, written as they were by the worker, were likely to cover this area of functioning in great detail.

Factors related to client-worker agreement based on the structured instrument

We explored the relationship between the following factors and client-worker agreement: beginning family functioning score, movement based on the Profile, relationship to worker, social class of client, and race of client.

We expected to find that the beginning level of functioning would have an impact upon the extent of agreement between worker and client. The greater the extent of problemicity, we reasoned, the greater the possibility that worker and client would view the situation differently, largely because of their differing frames of reference. The data, however, did not support this hypothesis. When we correlated client-worker agreement with beginning scores, we found the correlations to be low and statistically not significant for the main categories and for overall functioning.

Whether viewed as cause or effect, positive movement might be expected to go hand in hand with a close worker-client relationship which in turn might lead to freer communication and ultimately to a high level of agreement between the two. We correlated both movement and change in relationship to worker with client-worker agreement. A relatively high positive statistically significant association was found between overall positive movement as measured by the Profile and client-worker agreement (Gamma = +.539; chi square = 9.83, 2 d.f., p < .01).

The relationship between movement and client-worker agreement was considerably weaker for the separate areas of functioning, though positive in 7 of the 8 areas (the exception was the Use of Community Resources). Gammas for the seven areas ranged from +.060 in Child Care and Training to +.314 in Household Conditions and Practices, the latter being the only area in which the relationship was found to be statistically significant (Chi square = 8.75, 2 d.f., p < .02).

As to the second variable, we correlated change in Relationship to Worker with client-worker agreement and, as expected, found that the proportion of client-worker pairs who agreed on overall functioning was highest for pairs whose relationship had improved, next highest for those which remained at the same level, and lowest for pairs whose relationship had deteriorated (Gamma equal to +.518 and chi square of 7.07[8], 2 d.f., p < .05). The beginning level of client-worker relationship was found unrelated to the degree of agreement between the two.

Discrepancies in the social milieux of certain clients and workers have been alleged to result in differences in their perspectives that affect the relationship and ultimately the course of treatment.[9] If this were so, we would expect that worker and client would be less likely to agree when social discrepancies in social milieux are maximized. Since nearly all workers came from middle-class backgrounds and all but one was white, it was anticipated that congruence between worker and client would be greatest for those pairs in which the client was white and in the highest levels of social status (I-IV, modified Hollingshead). Neither hypothesis is supported by the data. Concerning social class, the reverse was true; a statistically significant[10] negative relationship was found between client-worker agreement and social class of client (Gamma = -.214; chi square = 13.07, 2 d.f., p < .01). No relationship at all was found between race of client and client-worker agreement.

Worker variability relative to agreement with clients

Sacks and his colleagues[11] had observed marked variation in the extent to which various workers were in accord with their clients. This suggested our final line of inquiry, and we also found that client-worker agreement in the assessment of client movement varied greatly among the eight FLIP workers. To determine this we calculated for each client-worker pair the percentage of items on which they agreed.[12]

For each worker we examined the percentage of cases in which agreement with the client was high (they responded similarly on more than 75% of the items). As shown below the range is from a low of no cases to a high of 95.5% of a caseload. The mean percent is 29.9. Using the code numbers assigned to workers in the previous chapter, workers are ranked below according to the percent of cases for which high agreement was found.

We further examined the correlation between the rank order of the workers based on rate of agreement and that based on rate of effectiveness (see Table 15, Chapter 7), and found a positive but statistically non-significant correlation between the two rank orders ($r_s = .429$)[13]. The findings, although far from conclusive, suggest that worker sensitivity and empathy are important factors in helping the client.

Worker	Percent of cases in which agreement was high	Total number of cases in which both client and worker filled out questionnaire*
1	95. 5	22
8	66. 7	18
3	30. 8	26
4	15. 8	19
2	12. 5	16
5	9. 1	11
6	8. 7	23
7	0. 0	19

*This number falls short of total caseload of worker.

Summarizing the findings resulting from this comparison of practitioner and client evaluation of movement based on a structured instrument, we note a high degree of agreement on overall functioning and in the main categories. The most typical pattern was agreement on positive change. Among client-worker pairs who disagreed about the direction of overall movement, the proportions of clients and workers making the more conservative judgment were about equal. In the main categories of functioning, clients tended to be slightly more positive than workers. As to which one in the pair is more conservative, our findings support neither the study by Crane[14] nor the one by Sacks.[15] Client-worker congruence was found highest in the category Economic Practices and Conditions and lowest in Social Activities. The relationships between the self-view and the worker's view of the client's movement as determined by the questionnaire and the Profile were generally positive but tended to be of a low to moderate order. Positive change in social functioning and in the client-worker relationship was found to be correlated with client-worker agreement. Social class was negatively associated and beginning score and ethnicity showed no relationship to agreement.

Consistent with the findings by Sacks et al.,[16] a great deal of variability was exhibited by the eight practitioners in the extent to which they agreed with their clients. In our own study it appears that workers seem to vary markedly in their sensitivity to what is taking place in their clients' lives. Thus, we found worker rank on rate of agreement to be positively but not significantly correlated with rank order on rate of effectiveness. We have provided additional though not powerful evidence that this sensitivity has some influence on practitioner effectiveness.

Finally, with respect to the conclusions of Sacks et al.[16], that agreement is positively correlated to the amount of information the worker possesses about the case, our data are ambiguous. On the one hand one finding--lowest agreement in the area of Social Activities and highest agreement in the category Economic Conditions and Practices--tends to support that interpretation. On the other hand, the finding that the greatest discrepancy between client self-judgment and Profile assessment occurred in Child Care and Training, an area in which the worker had extensive information, is contrary to the interpretation provided by Sacks and associates.

Notes

1. John Crane, Louis Reimer, and Susan Poulos, An Experiment in the Deployment of Welfare Aides, Research Department, Children's Aid Society of Vancouver, British Columbia, June 1970, p. 27; Elizabeth Most, "Measuring Change in Marital Satisfaction," Social Work, Vol. 9, No. 3, July 1964, pp. 64-70; Joel G. Sacks, Panke M. Bradley, and Dorothy Fahs Beck, Client's Progress Within Five Interviews, Family Service Association of America, New York, 1970; pp. 52-81.

2. The same procedure of calculating mean area and total scores to represent the client's assessment of change was used to determine that of the worker.

3. The procedure for creating an index of agreement consisted simply of cross-tabulating the mean scores described above of the worker total and area scores with those of the client. Code numbers were then assigned as follows (the two categories of positive change were combined into one):

1-Worker and client agree that negative change took place. (Both obtained mean area or total scores of 1.0-2.7.)

2-Worker and client agree that no change took place. (Both obtained mean area or total scores of 2.8-3.2)

3-Worker and client agree that positive change took place. (Both obtained mean area or total scores of 3.3 or greater.)

4-The client's assessment of change was more positive than the worker. This encompasses two situations: The client thought that improvement had taken place but worker's assessment was that either no change had occurred or that the situation had worsened; the client thought that no change had occurred and the worker viewed the situation as having worsened.

5-The worker's assessment of change was more positive than the client's. This encompasses the two possibilities described above under code number 4, except that worker and client occupy reverse positions.

For use in the cross-tabulations, the five categories were dichotomized to represent "agreement" (1 to 3) and "disagreement" (4,5).

4. Most, loc. cit.

5. Sacks, et al. , op. cit.

6. Sacks, op. cit.

7. We were unable to apply chi square as a test of statistical significance to most of the data in this section of the analysis since the tables contained too many cells in which the expected frequency was less than 5. Instead, we relied upon gamma to assess the strength of the relationship among factors.

8. The relationship was found to be statistically significant but the use of the chi square test is questionable, for the table contained 2 cells in which the expected frequencies were less than 5.

9. This issue is dealt with in the articles and books listed in note 6, Chapter 6.

10. The appropriateness of using chi square is questionable because the tables contained one cell in which the expected frequency is less than 5.

11. Sacks, et al. , op. cit.

12. We obtained the percentage by simply counting the number of items on which worker and client agreed and dividing by the total number of items both client and worker answered. If either client or worker failed to answer or responded "not applicable", the item was omitted from the base. In computing the percentages we collapsed "better" and "much better" and "worse" and "much worse" into single categories of "better" and "worse", respectively.

13. The Spearman rank order correlation of .429 fell below the .643 needed to reach statistical significance at the .05 level. It should be noted that the correlation failed to reach statistical significance primarily because of the discrepancy in the ranking of a single worker on the two dimensions. Of the 8 workers, 3 had identical ranks, another 3 were 1 rank apart, 1 was 3 ranks apart and the one worker referred to above was 6 positions away, or nearly at opposite ends on the two dimensions.

14. Crane, op. cit.

15. Sacks, et al. , op. cit.

16. Sacks, et al. , op. cit.

INDEX

231

17-18, 103; see also
Family Functioning;
Movement